I Never Sang
for
My Mother

a Memoir

Betty Walter

Publication 2016

Edited by Marcia Gleckler & John Hutchinson

Front cover photo--John Hutchinson
"The Adirondacks"

CONTENTS

TO THE FUTURE

These musings, mullings and meditations are dedicated to my three grandchildren: Campbell Walter Miller, Jake Henry Miller and Mattalin Georgia Miller. Many years from now, when they reach adulthood, my hope is that they will find in my reflections some key to better understanding a part of their own family history. The first section covers the first twenty-two years. The next section will focus, not on brief memory pictures, but more on short essays dealing with people, places, incidents and responses that contributed, for good or ill, to where I stand at sixty-five. This effort, initiated by a genuine desire to leave behind a testament about my "trip" for my sons, Douglas and Kenneth, and for their children, has had some far-reaching effects. Last year, my class of people (aged 65-80) joined forces with a talented group of young writers at the Carver School of Arts to share their writing. What emerged from that experience was far more important than words. The old and the young found that friendship and respect has nothing to do with spiked hair, earrings, walkers or wrinkles. It has to do with a willingness to transcend the exterior and accept the interior.

This is my gift to the future.

Elizabeth Floyd Walker

This is the use of memory:
for liberation – not less of love but expanding
of love beyond desire, and so liberation
from the future, as well as the past.

T.S. Eliot, *Four Quartets*

Storytelling, you know,
has a real function. The process of the storytelling is itself a
healing process, partly because you have someone there who is
taking the time to tell you a story that has great meaning to
them. They're taking the time to do this because your life could
use some help, but

they don't want to come over and just
give advice. They want to give it to you in a form that becomes
inseparable from your whole self. That's what stories do. Stories
differ from advice in that, once you get them, they become a
fabric of your whole soul. That is why they heal you.

Alice Walker
1990 interview in *Common Boundary*

A FEW EARLY MEMORY PICTURES

I was seven years old. Grandfather Harry Walter was the new occupant of the bed in the front bedroom. An enormous man, his form under the mound of covers looked so different from the slender outline of the bed's last occupant: my mother. Harry was a gruff man who had sold a department store in Detroit when he started to ail from something that would kill him in less than a year. This snapshot revolves around the grandfather I had never seen, and a Pinocchio doll that he brought to me as a token of his esteem. He handed me the doll which resided in a shoe box. The doll was wooden, there was a short red jacket, blue shorts and knee-high socks. But it was the nose that got me! I tried to be the nice-nice girl that training and circumstances had labeled me, but instead, I started to cry. Great gift! Now that I think of it, this doll and his estranged wife's teddy bear caused some reaction (chemical!) that stirred up my tear ducts. I ran into my room (which happened to be separated from the sick bay by only a door), and hid the Pinocchio doll in my closet. Before I did, I turned him around so I would never have to look at the elongated nose. Instead of a monster in the closet, I harbored a piece of wood with a long, sharp nose that I wanted to break off. He also had a cute little hat with a feather on it. I threw that away. In my defense, let me say that I was devoted to my Betsy Wetsy doll. Give her a bottle of water and she always performed. In fact, I think Betsy Wetsy resides in a box in the basement. I wonder if she still works?

On my first day of first grade at the Glen Burnie Elementary School, Mrs. Smoot, a tall, angular woman with prominent teeth, stood in front of forty six-year-olds. The room smelled strongly of the oil used in cleaning the ancient wooden floors. The desks were cramped, the room was cramped, my stomach felt cramped. Therefore, I quickly decided this gig was not my style. I already knew how to read, and I certainly was not interested in the 2 + 2 routine. Now that I look back, that was an early sign of future problems! I squirmed and pulled at a horrible, big red bow affixed to my hair. I think I lost the bow that day. When I heard recess, I thought home, and made tracks from the playground and up the street to safety. Mrs. Smoot sounded a red alert, her seventh grade son cut me off at the pass, and I was escorted back to prison. Today, whenever I half-kiddingly say, "I want to run away," I remember the time I made the unsuccessful attempt. Maybe some people are not designed for breakaways.

This is the picture of Betty and the Rabbit. Like all children, I longed for a pet. After much whining, my father finally conceded that a bunny beat a puppy anytime. Well, maybe! My only pet connection prior to Peter were my two ducks, Peter and Puddle. They quacked and waddled but weren't good in the unconditional love department. Naturally, I didn't have the foggiest concept about how to care for a pet, but I did know I wanted something warm and fuzzy and pettable. The bunny was bought, the cage was placed outside and my dreams that night were filled with visions of Peter and Betty gamboling around the back yard. Daylight broke and I lunged for the window to make sure Peter was still caged. A carrot seemed appropriate for our first encounter. I crept downstairs, procured the carrot and dashed outdoors to bond with the bunny. He nibbled at the carrot and seemed ready, if not especially willing, to have an adventure. I sprung the lock, took Peter by the ears and swung him not too gently as I skipped to the back door. Why I thought Peter would be tolerated in the house still eludes me. I pulled the screen door open; it connected with Peter's head. Kaboom. I looked down at Peter. Needless to say, he was limp. My memory of dropping the bunny and racing around the house, screaming, remains vivid in my picture album.

THOSE VISITS TO HUNTINGTON, MARYLAND

My father was the once-a-week dentist in Huntington, a small town in southern Maryland. Friday was dentist day, and every Friday all summer long I went with him. The office had two rooms and a tiny porch outside, a drill that worked by his foot pumping the pedal, making a whirring sound, a telephone with a hand crank on the right that required the caller to crank before the operator said "Number, please," and old National Geographic magazines for patients to peruse while they waited for the whir: all are memories I carry of that office. But it was the house next door that was a Friday haven for me.

The Gibson's owned and operated the lumber yard that bordered the house. Mrs. Gibson was ample of bosom, of waist and, far more importantly, of heart. She baked wonderful cookies, the milk was always cold, and the radio was always on. In the afternoon, we listened to the fifteen-minute soaps: "Stella Dallas, Backstage Wife," "Lorenzo Jones" and his wife, Belle, "Portia Faces Life," and "Jack Armstrong, All-American Boy." I got hooked on those brief encounters with lives far more exciting than mine. Mrs. Gibson was hooked, but good! Even her live-in sister, Edith, who was "different," sat quietly and listened.

Edith, who was as we say today, "mentally challenged," always wore a freshly pressed house dress and had the unpleasant duty of catching and killing the chicken my father bought from her each Friday. I presume, rather than egg money, Edith got beheading money. I was fascinated with the chase, Edith, ax in hand, the catch, the squawking (the chicken, not me) and the blood that shot out when ax found neck. She then proceeded to de-feather the bird and used paraffin wax to make the feathers go faster. Whenever I buy chicken parts, chicken whole, chicken cooked, chicken cold, or any of the varieties of chickens sold, I remember Edith and her ax. Well, truthfully, I don't always think of Edith, but I do remember that she would play croquet with me and I always won. I do not know if this was due to innate kindness or the fact that she was "different." I do know that my forages into Huntington were happy times.

Today, this once tiny dot is a large suburban sprawl with many malls, mini marts, and maximum protection for the inhabitants. I do not know what they are being protected from. I do know that sometimes I long for the Huntington of old. No, I will not say "the good old days." But, I will say that playing by myself in the corn fields in the back of the house, pumping water from the pump, sitting under the enormous oak tree and spinning imaginary tales where I was always the damsel in distress and the knight was just around the bend, hold a certain appeal as I approach Social Security. Why can't we "Go Home Again," Thomas Wolfe?

A DOG NAMED POOCHIE

After the untimely death of Peter Rabbit, it took a long winter racked with diseases passed around in second grade before I finally wore my father down. I think it was after being quarantined with scarlet fever that he finally gave up and caved in. I did have a long spell abed to work the "If I ever get better, could I please, please, please have a doggie." The "If" always works. Conditions were set. The pooch could not be big, shed or bark. Sounded more like a cat to me, but I was willing to go along with anything. We found what looked to be the perfect pet with some dog lady who bred fox terriers. Actually, my father named the pooch "Poochie."

I must have been on a down slide mentally since I didn't know that pooch meant dog and putting the 'ie' on just meant girl dog. Anyway, Poochie she was and Poochie she remained. Not possessing long ears, I could not swing her and that was a break for the new pet. Maybe girl dogs are, or were, as anxious to please as girl/humans were in those long-ago times. Poochie did not shed (she was bristled, not furred), she was tiny (seven pounds, nine ounces) and she was scared enough of my father that barking became a distant memory for her as she approached adolescence. Like all God's children, she had her likes and dislikes.

Poochie was very fond of boy dogs, and may I say, they returned the affection. Was defeminizing doggies not an option in those times? I don't know because Poochie never visited either the general dog doctor or the dog gynecologist. She should have. Although mothering was not Poochie's long suit, she thoroughly enjoyed (or so it would seem) the process needed for reproduction. Like good catholic women before the advent of the pill or the onset of the feminist movement, she had three liters of little pooches at regular intervals. I learned a lot about conning unsuspecting parents of friends into taking the products. Here is where my salesmanship skills were honed. Many of those pups were somewhat peculiar looking since she was attracted to boy dogs not necessarily in the terrier family. Once the birthing was attended to, Poochie lost interest in any of the feeding, nuzzling and licking needed. My Aunt Bessie would bottle feed the babies, cursing all the while. Poochie, free again, would trot out for new adventures around the block! I adored Poochie and she returned the adoration by coming to the hated schoolhouse daily to trot me home, appearing at just the moment the piano lesson was over, and always being overjoyed to see me even after a brief absence.

When I left for Hannah Moore, Poochie took up new lodgings with a family who ran a general store outside of Huntington. They sold products in barrels, cheese in hunks and big saltines that I haven't seen in years. Once I went down to see my old and always loyal friend. I had not touched paws with Poochie for three or four years. The once skinny "sexually active" girl's best friend had gotten very fat. Her legs were still skinny, so walking was a chore. Her eyesight was failing but her memory had not dimmed. She labored up from her blanket by a barrel, waddled as fast as she was able over to me, and tried, unsuccessfully, to stand on her hind legs. She had not forgotten. Now that my knees are beginning to creak, my weight is a worry, and I seem to spend as much time on top of the feather mattress and the down comforter that encase my bed as I do between the feathers, I long for Poochie.

HUTZLER'S: A MONUMENT TO CIVILITY

During the 1940's and for some time beyond, Hutzler's on Howard Street was a monument to civility, service, good taste and, always, good manners. I loved Hutzler's, the sixth floor dining room replete with starched white tablecloths, sparkling napkins, chicken salad never to be equaled and chocolate sundaes rivaled only by Marconi's. Elegant women modeled elegant clothes, all of which could be found on the third floor--Better Dresses, of course. Sales personnel stayed from the time they were young until middling old age came unexpectedly and suddenly they were retired. Packages bought could either be delivered at home by the next day at no charge or sent in some mysterious way to the connected parking garage. An attendant brought the car from the parked car realms above, a ticket produced the waiting purchases, the narrow garage passageway to Saratoga Street had to be driven slowly, and honking was suggested. Nothing was demanded, just honk--if it's not too much trouble.

A rite of passage was the first permanent wave in Hutzler's salon on the fifth floor. Patients were sent to individual cubicles and the sizzle machine was brought in. Hanging by varying lengths of electric cord were small to large clasps that had the power to fry innocent heads. I lost my braids, gleefully threw away the braid bows and began my passage to young womanhood. I went in looking like Margaret O'Brien and came out looking like a most imperfect Shirley Temple.

WWII STARTED AT THE MOVIES

I learned that the Japanese had bombed Pearl Harbor while attending my usual Sunday afternoon movie matinee with my father. I remember the movie: one of the road films with Bob Hope, Bing Crosby and a saronged Dorothy Lamour. No one remembers plot. It was cold that Sunday in Baltimore and the announcement frightened me. My father was distracted and a plane flew over later that evening in the landing pattern at Friendship Airport. I can today call up the fear I experienced. Was a bomb about to be dropped? As a singularly lonely child with a highly developed imagination, I was forever weaving plots and open to expectations of catastrophe.

In the way of all ironies, I first heard about the bombing at the movies, and for the rest of the real war learned about it through the unreality of Hollywood. John Wayne personified all that was truly American, Van Johnson died beautifully, Veronica Lake defied the enemy, hand grenade held high in a forgotten film. She was, of course, an army nurse. The extras all had oriental faces. I fell in love with William Holden. Clark Gable never stirred my heart but he and Lana Turner did more than one turn in the celluloid world of forbidden love among bombs. I wanted to grow up to be Mrs. Miniver. I wanted Walter Pidgeon to be my husband. Was ever there a man so kind? Was ever there a woman as beautiful as Greer Garson? Was ever there a war so romanticized on film?

MISS ZEMAN AND THE KUETHE LIBRARY

Pat Reynolds and I always got to the Kuethe Library ten minutes before starting time. Every Monday, Wednesday and Friday night, the double doors were opened by Miss Zeman at exactly seven p.m. and closed tightly at nine on the nose. As I recall, those were the only hours this magic kingdom offered us the opportunity to travel to exotic places, to lose ourselves in Nancy Drew and to long to have a dog named Lassie. Miss Zeman, a secretary by day, became our fellow conspirator by night. She directed us to shelves with writers we did not yet know, guided us gently to poets not allowed in elementary schools, and as our curiosity increased, moved us from the large children's section to the not-so-large young adult offerings. After that, we found the adult books ourselves.

In those days before the birth of television and the death of radio soap operas, Pat and I became experienced travelers of the Southwest with the help of Zane Grey, we flew from being twelve to becoming seventeen using the images of Maureen Daly's "Seventeenth Summer" as our plane, and we row-boated into the as yet uncharted waters of passion using Walt Whitman's words as our map.

Whenever I smell a musty room, I remember the Kuethe Library. After Miss Zeman unlocked the doors, she opened the windows with the hook at the end of a long pole. But, the smell never really receded. Now, when I go into a supermarket library, I long to find a book that will transport me into unknown territory, open a door I never knew existed, or stir my imagination so my fancy takes flight. Occasionally, I look over my shoulder hoping to find Miss Zeman once again. She seems to have vanished forever.

SATURDAY NIGHT: GLEN BURNIE

When my mother went to Trudeau in Saranac Lake, New York to valiantly battle her tuberculosis, Aunt Bessie, my father's sister, signed on board as "keeper." I've tried to find a word to describe her assignment from the time I was seven until I was eleven, but "keeper" seems to cover all the angles. Bess "kept house" (an ancient expression as well as a concept one no longer hears today), kept the kitchen smelling of chickens roasting, cakes baking and bacon frying, and kept Betty clean, quiet, and reasonably obedient. In all fairness, she was not a mean person. Bess (according to my father and her sister Maude) had been born unhappy, ran on anger, and fed on her resentments of people past and present who had done-her-wrong. Since there was a lengthy list of wrong doers, she always had a lot to think about! She went back to Baltimore on weekends to touch base with Gloria and Maude, and returned on Monday morning to take up the reins of keeper duties.

This snapshot is a Saturday night that I remember as though it were yesterday. I do not know where my father was, but I hope he was having a good time! It was bitter cold, and Bess and I went to the Glen Theater (where else?) to see a movie. On the way back, we stopped at the neighborhood pub so I could put a nickel in the claw machine. I clawed a treasure: a plastic bracelet with little figures hanging from it. The finest jewels could not have delighted me more. We each got a bittersweet chocolate candy bar, a movie magazine and marshmallows to put on top of the promised hot chocolate.

When we got home, Bessie made a fire in the fireplace (something she generally scorned), stirred up the best hot chocolate I have ever tasted, broke open the bittersweet bars and then we had the greatest treat of all, listening to some kid's radio quiz show where the listeners sent in questions. A miracle: One of the three questions I had sent in was used! Bess was laughing and congratulatory. This was fun! Even when I jumped up and spilled the hot chocolate all over myself and the chair, she didn't

14

plug in the anger cord. Although I can never remember Bess hugging me, I have always remembered this brief moment in time when a plastic bracelet that cost five cents, a cup of spilled hot chocolate and Bess laughing spelled happiness. I also know now that like most of us, Bess did the best she could. Maybe what all of us should keep in mind is that the finest epitaph may be: She Tried.

SUNDAY EVENINGS: GLEN BURNIE 1939-1944

At seven o'clock, Jack Benny came over the airwaves. My father and I went to a movie in Baltimore every Sunday afternoon. I loved Sundays. The day that can seem endless now was that "long awaited but always expected something we live for." My love affair with the silver screen started early and has continued unabated ever since. But, the very best part of Sundays was when we got home, started a fire in the fireplace if the weather permitted, called Poochie up from the basement, popped corn over the fire and listened to Jack insult Rochester. I can't remember what came on after Jack, but he taught me the joy of laughter. Since I still believe that's the best medicine ever invented, I owe him a tremendous debt of gratitude. I now realize how fortunate I was that only the wireless existed at this point in time. My imagination was sharpened, my ears attuned to hear the nuances, and my eyes were mercifully left to their own devices. No pretty, or ugly, pictures to spell the story out, explain the laughter or deaden the senses. My drug of choice at that time was my imagination. What a wonderful drug it was! Now, when I spend mindless hours watching the pictures on the tube float in front of me, feel my senses deadening, and my spirit shriveling, some small voice inside cries, "Jack Benny, where are you?" There is no answer.

THE GLEN BURNIE CARNIVAL

Pure joy. When I was maybe six or seven, merely the anticipation of carnival made my heart beat fast, my dreams resound with the sound of calliope music and my hopes hinge on being lucky enough to win a kewpie doll if the wheel settled on my number. If I could paint, which, trust me, I cannot, I would paint you a picture of the sawdust, the Ferris wheel, the many games of chance, the bumper cars and my favorite of all, the magic horses that whirled around and around and always seemed to slow down close to the place where one mounted the steed. Before I could cavort at the carnival unattended (probably around eight) my father would take me and always be waving every time the painted horse flew by. I remember him smiling; I would wave and smile back. That was the golden ring. Ah-ha. And, there it is.

OLIVE DUNKER, A FRIEND

My girlfriend, Olive Dunker, had what we would call "big hair" today. That is to say, she had what appeared to me to be an endless sea of long curls that bounced when she walked and stood out behind her when she ran. Not by nature a luster, I longed for those curls, I hated those curls, I loved those curls, I wanted those curls. It's the same old story. My hair was straight, to me unbearably uninteresting, and I always wore bangs which I also loathed. One day, tiring of the endless Monopoly games we played through the endless summers we shared, I suggested that we play "hairdresser." We secluded ourselves in Olive's room, found a pair of scissors, and proceeded to hone our skill. Olive nipped at my bangs, I nipped at one of Olive's curls. I suggested she remove the bow that was always clamped to the right side of her ten ride-side curls. Without the barrette under the bow, the ten curls fell forward. Seconds later, there were only nine curls. The missing one lay on the floor. Olive, by nature a sweet child, started to howl. Mother Olive rushed in and started to cry. The deed was done. Within minutes, Mother Olive was able to twirl the nine remaining curls so that the bare clump of hair was covered. No one would ever see the damage. Within a short amount of time, we were back at the Monopoly board and the curl was placed in the middle of a book, I presume for safekeeping. Olive and I remained Monopoly and movie friends, although the game of hairdresser never came up again.

CHRISTMAS IN LAKE PLACID: 1939-1943

From age seven to eleven, Christmas was spent in the rarified atmosphere of Lake Placid in upstate New York. Now known because of Olympic events, it was at that time a haven for skiers, skaters, dog sled enthusiasts and tubercular patients not confined to state hospitals. My mother belonged to the latter group. For one magical week each of these five years, I was transported by my father and the Baltimore and Ohio Railroad into a wonderland of frigid air, endless snow, sleigh bells that actually rang around the necks of horses whose breath wheezed and formed a greyish mist, and a team of dogs running in unison across the frozen lake pulling yet another sled with blanketed people. No canned music, hee-hawing Santas or commercials seducing children into the land of I Want. The memory remains frozen and, in the way of many memories, has never varied over the decades.

These trips began with boarding a train from Penn Station in Baltimore and riding to New York in the lounge car. Single arm chairs that swirled, porters, always smiling, forever kind, brought cokes and coffee and hidden goodies for young children. Swirling, reading and watching the scenery flash by while encased in comfort is a feeling I have never recaptured. The greatest joy, however, was ahead. The Pullman car with the heavy green drapes sectioning off each bunk had an allure I have never forgotten. There was a certain smell that lingers in memory. Was this the odor of nightly sleepers behind heavy drapes? The clacking sound of the train as it sped along endless miles of track, barely open blinds that allowed me to glimpse fields and lighted villages in the distance, was an experience I cherish. Thus began my love affair with trains. The dining car with starched white linen tablecloths and accompanying napkins was part of the memory. The train ran smoothly, no food spilled, no porter swayed. Perhaps that is one of memory's tricks. Everything stays in place.

Sleep was induced by the sound of wheels striking track. The mournful whistle that permeated the darkness only added to my pleasure. A green mesh hammock that held "whatever's" over the bunk fascinated me. Once, on a return trip, I left a pen and pencil set deep in the crevices of mesh. Although I wrote in indecipherable childish scrawl, a letter to Mr. B & O Railroad, I received no reply.

I remember on one of those five magical musical tours arriving in Lake Placid when the thermometer read thirty below zero. A bunny fur jacket, furred hat and bunny muff did their duty in warding off frostbite. Porters scurried with luggage, cabs waited with heaters roaring, and the lake--iced fifty feet downward--beckoned. That might have been the Christmas my mother gave me a skating outfit. Although never qualifying as a figure-eighter, I plugged around the enormous rink. What I lacked in skill, I made up for in determination. My father always watched from the sidelines. Now, when I think of sidelines, I always see my father watching.

We bundled up in the sled behind the frothing horses. My mother had neither the desire nor the energy to accompany us on any of these adventures. One time, the dog sled driver let me stand on the driver tracks, hold the whip and call out "gee-haw" or whatever passed for dog commands. Joy! Another thought occurs to me as I recall those postcard Christmases over fifty-five years ago. The "we" in my childhood always meant my father and me. My mother, wracked by coughing, could never become part of the we.

Unaware of the politics of sidelining, I experienced a joy that belongs only to children. It never occurred to me, nor does it now, that a hotel room was an unusual set for childhood holidays. A real tree, small, appeared. Presents came from some undiscovered place, carols were sung by real carolers and Lake Placid Hotel became a fairyland of glitter and bells, warmth and reunions. But, most importantly, it was family. Through some process of osmosis, I learned early that families are fragile and none fit unreal technicolored fantasy woven in children's books and Hollywood movies of that time. Even then, I knew no family named Walton.

Decades later and a lifetime removed from the train's whistle, the crunch of packed snow, the dogs dancing across Lake Placid, the aborted attempts at skiing and the pride involved in staying upright on laced skates, I remember those Christmases with great love. In memory, I hear the sleigh bells ringing. In reality, I see the connection with my mother, the love my father gave to me, and the never-ending imprint of a family's history written into each of our final chapters.

ZACH DID NOT WALK, HE SWAYED

When I was ten years old, I walked an extra mile each morning, not for a camel, but to "pick up" my friend Celeste Turner. Overtly, we liked to walk to school together. Covertly, my reason for the additional hike was to catch a brief glimpse of her older brother Zach. Zach, four years older and a high school freshman, did not walk, he swayed. A town-renowned dancer, he took jitterbugging to an art form. His carefully coiffed pompadour never wavered in the wind, his smile ignited and excited, and his bevy of teen dancers cloistered around him in hopes of being one of the chosen to wiggle and shimmy her way across the floor in his company. Jitterbugging was the forties teen response to parents who remained rooted in the waltz.

When I went away to boarding school, I glimpsed Zach only during the summers. When I was thirteen, Zach worked in the local drugstore, and the summer of '46 was my summer of many cokes. Once, I stayed until the closing hour—nine o'clock. Sweet time at the counter sipping while I fed nickels into the brightly colored music machine. Once, Zach walked with me to my home, a short block-and-a-half away, but I preferred to think he "walked me home." "Goodnight, sleep tight. Don't let the bedbugs bite" was his admonishment as I walked across Crain Highway. My heart stood still following the dictates of the song-of-the-times.

During my fifteenth summer, I saw Zach only once. He was a college man then, majoring in pharmacy, but was meant to always dance, to forever fly without benefit of wings, and to be surrounded by that bevy of flying footed girls through eternity.

When the fateful time arrived that all dateless girls dread, the senior prom, neither my friend, Miffie, nor I had any prospects. Heeding Lady MacBeth's credo to "screw your courage to the sticking point," I not only invited Zach, now an almost pharmacist, but dared to ask that he bring a dancing partner for

Miffie. They came. Dressed in blue with matching elbow length gloves that constantly itched, and ill-fitting, dyed-to-match blue shoes, I stumbled when Zach dipped, prayed that the music would never pick up speed, and tried to think of something to talk about; this was not magic. What it was was the beginning of my discovery that fantasy princes should never be invited to the ball. They are best left encased in juke boxes.

When I went to college, I met other and more accessible princes. Because I saw them daily none of them ever inspired the depths of longing and admiration that Zach did.

Three years ago, I learned that Zach had died of AIDS. I felt an encasing sadness that had nothing to do with juke boxes but a great deal to do with the knowledge gleaned over decades that there are no princes and Cinderella's shoe is never really returned.

AUNT MAUDE WAS FUN AND FUNNY

Aunt Maude, the youngest of the Walter girls, took on the mantle of 'baby girl' and ran with it. Tiny in stature, she easily fit the part. Her voice was soft, and she had a tendency to look lost. Thus, everyone wanted to come to her rescue. In reality, she was the one who provided the glue, the stability and the comfort of her person to members of the clan. She possessed an innate ability to listen, not judge too harshly, and to keep her mouth tightly clamped. But, perhaps her greatest gift was her humor. Maude was fun, and funny--a combination devoutly to be wished for.

Often, I visited her apartment on Gwynns Falls Parkway. As a child, I played in the bedroom. Taking out her small assortment of dresses, I became a world renowned buyer for all fancy dress shops in New York City. I remember one dress in particular, blue with white polka dots. I often sold this to queens around the world. Lest this be misunderstood, these were queens with crowns and their own throne, with a reasonably real king standing at attention off in the distance.

There was a tiny kitchen that I adored. There, I played housekeeper, cook and cleaner-upper. Unhappily, I did not carry that game into adulthood. Reality never compares to the fanciful kingdoms created by children. There is a line from one of my favorite plays, "Harvey," that I always remember of Elwood P. Dowd who defends his imaginary friend--a six-foot rabbit named Harvey--in the following manner: "I have wrestled with reality for over forty years, and I finally won out over it." Good for Elwood.

Halfway down the long, dark hallway was a cast iron door ensconced in the wall. A drop for garbage, the smell was overpowering, but the sound of the egg shells, coffee grounds, and pork chop bones being speeded to their resting place fascinated me. Having just become aware of Edgar Allen Poe, this was a perfect prop for the macabre tales spun in my mind's eye but never mercifully committed to page.

When I reached unchaperoned status at Hannah More for travel into the city, Aunt Maude was my contact person. Mary and Miffie would happily accompany me to Maudie's apartment. She provided a safe place, a concept none of us could have understood at the time. More importantly, she made us laugh, and we made her laugh...and we were happy.

Maude married Harry Shipley when she was in her thirties. Harry worked for the B&O Railroad. Unfortunately, he never discovered Harvey or a reasonable facsimile. Having courted for years, Harry and Maude were married secretly by the local parish priest. Secrets were big in our clan but all paled in comparison to the Shipley saga.

Mother Shipley loomed large in Harry's life. Father Shipley had understandably disappeared over the horizon when Harry was still in knickers. Thus, Harry assumed the child, father and husband role. Mother Shipley took to her bed, and enjoyed this prop for over thirty years. Harry, fearful his marriage would bring the angel of death to Mama's door, did not reveal his fall into darkness. For years, he went to his mother's house early each morning to stoke the coal furnace and not only fixed dinner for her each evening, but stayed to eat. She did not discover that Harry had married until the birth of her grandchild, Donald.

Donald Shipley, now in his fifties, is a most successful man who never forgot what little Maude did for him. She gave him the greatest gift of all. When Donald graduated from high school Maude forced him to go to the University of North Carolina on full scholarship. She could stoke her own furnace and fix her own dinner while poor Harry played with his year-round train set that circled the living room floor. Donald left, unwillingly, the sound of the forever running choo-choo trains, the plaintive whistle of the engine, and the presence of Harry, conductor's cap perched jauntily on his head, dreaming dreams of where those trains might take him.

When Maude was a few years over sixty, Harry toppled over one night after supper, "and it was all over." Maude seemed like a little ship without a rudder, compass or destination. Occasionally, miracles happen. Somehow, she was directed to St. Joseph's hospital in Towson. Down to ninety pounds, low on valium, high on anxiety and without sufficient funds to meet the meager monthly budget, she found that paradise that Harry had been seeking for decades.

The good nuns knew a cause when they saw one. Still enwrapped in their long black dresses, winged white headgear and rosaries clinking around their waists, they adopted Maude. Little Maudie became the weekend overseer for the nursing candidates. She lived at the hospital from Thursday through Monday, became adored by the girls, loved by the nuns, and admired by the medical staff. What she brought to her position could never be found in a textbook, taught in a class or ingested in a workshop. Her innate kindness, long buried sense of fun, and genuine interest in people, propelled her into twelve years of wonderful. Donald insisted his mother move in with him. For a year, Maude lived with Donald, his two girls and the wife Diane. After that year, Maude, with Don's help, moved to her own apartment. There she provided the same safe haven for her grand girls that she had fashioned in Baltimore. An unlikely savior, she brought to her old age the same qualities evidenced in her youth.

Maude is proof that ultimately we will be judged, and then remembered, for what we have given to others. She has given of herself, and that gift will continue in the hearts of all the people she has touched.

ELLEN, RED NAILS AND PALL MALL CIGARETTES

When I think of Ellen, I envision red nails, Pall Mall cigarettes, two yellowed, nicotine fingers on her right hand and a beauty that defied her status as a nurse and overshadowed her Delta roots. Not that nurses aren't beautiful, but Ellen carried herself with an elegance that turned the heads of men, but not their hearts. Entering the University of Maryland School of Nursing a few years before my mother, she was acclaimed as the best nurse in the city of Baltimore. Like so many people, she had two distinct personas: nurse and the woman. The woman never quite lived up to the aura of the nurse.

Shortly after Ellen, degreed and capped, graduated from nursing school, she met some very wealthy folks who were to become major players in her life: the McCormick's, of spice fame, and the Davis's, who did more than dabble in paint. I listened, wide-eyed, and open-eared to Ellen recounting the soap opera sagas of how even the very rich and very religious can fall from grace. No one knew I was eavesdropping. I was a good hider!

Ellen became part of the Davis family. Holidays were spent with the Davis tribe and they would frequently take her on twice-yearly trips to New York. If memory serves, the theater was verboten. Ballet and opera were acceptable. One, in either French or Italian, was impossible to understand; the other featured thin, ethereal women on their toes in tutus, most of whom died beautifully by the end of Act 1. Ellen proclaimed her love of the opera while taking me to the stage show and movie at the Hippodrome in Baltimore. She loved the vaudeville atmosphere of the cavernous theater on Eutaw Street. So did I. I never believed for a moment that she cared for opera.

Ellen's taste for money and the comforts therein was whetted during her many years as "friend" of the rich but not so famous. Her dream was to marry a wealthy doctor, hardly an uncommon fantasy. Oral family history entailed many engagements but no weddings.

Sometime after age fifty, Ellen signed on as a private duty nurse to an elderly gentleman by the name of Miller who had "married well," an expression no longer in use. His very wealthy wife had died at a fairly early age. Ellen signed on to be nurse overseer, party planner and a surrogate lady-of-the-manor. This could have been a match made on mutually beneficial land. Ellen would have excelled as the force at the manor, and her nursing, tending and planning skills were the perfect resume for the job.

The future seemed rich, if not rosy. One Christmas Eve, Ellen chaperoned the young Miller son into Baltimore to shop along Charles Street for suitable gifts. At that time Charles Street was akin to Rodeo Drive: fancy shops, dress emporiums, displays of jewels in windows with bars, and mink coats, stoles and muffs worn by pale androgynous manikins. Charles Street gave us commoners a window view of how the "Old Baltimore" residents shopped. Buses ran on time transporting old ladies who could no longer drive or afford to be driven back to Roland Park. Sonny Miller stepped in front of one these buses at the corner of Charles and Mulberry and ended not only his life but any dreams of "manordom" that Ellen harbored. She looked up for one moment. Sonny looked down and the bus scrambled the script.

Shortly after this scrambling, Ellen moved back to her home across from Memorial Stadium. She did other private duty nursing long-term contracts in the homes of the wealthy, shorter stints in homes where the patient died sooner than expected. She was the first person called when private duty was needed and the client had the money for this luxury. Today, we have giant warehouses built to accommodate countless people kept alive due to the marvels of modern medicine. There's money in them thar pills.

Ellen never found "happy." I doubt that she even found content. When Thoreau wrote "The mass of men lead lives of quiet desperation," he must have had all the Ellens in mind. Like so many, she longed for that unattainable something that was never there.

AUNT BESSIE, A BAT OUT OF HELL

Aunt Bessie Blasini came on board The-Big-House-in-Glen-Burnie the day after my mother left for Lake Placid in yet another search for the cure. Tuberculosis was the enemy; cold air, rest and sound nutrition were being hailed as the friend. For the next four-and-a-half years, mother fought the good fight as best she could, and Aunt Bessie waged her own private battle as resident housekeeper.

The morning Bess arrived, I was in bed with an ailment that had a tubercular in front of it and, if memory serves correctly, a meningitis followed the "T" word. Bess bounded up the stairs yelling, "Here I come, a bat out of hell." Little did I know how prophetic those words would be!

My father was in desperate need of not only a keeper of the house, but also a keeper of his one and only, me. He was unaware that soon his long absent father, Harry, would claim the bed relinquished by my mother, and Bess would also be assigned the role of "caretaker" for the father she had been taught to loathe. Harry had danced the light fantastic out of Hinton, West Virginia, leaving behind one wife, three daughters and one son, who became by default the titular head of the household.

The family's financial legacy was a bankrupt bar aptly named "Walter's Saloon." Prior to falling in love with long distance, Harry had enjoyed his libation of beer. Bess had been weaned on tales of Papa's matching two for Harry with one for each customer, and in my recollection she consistently treated the dying Harry with poorly concealed disdain. In fairness, I know that seven-year-olds are not adept at forecasting Bess's moods and the undercurrents that could bring on the tidal waves of her anger.

My father always said that Bess was born angry. Of the three sisters, she was the least pretty, the most aggressive and the only one who could take on the keeping and caring job. Bess loved to cook; believed that cleanliness was right up there with godliness and actually seemed to enjoy scrubbing the clothes on the scrub board and then, after many rinses, wringing them through the manual wringer with a dedication that bordered on vengeance. No doubt those versed in psychological punditry today would see all sorts of transference going through that wringer.

Bess was never "mean" to me. When she and my father locked horns, I always escaped upstairs, or downstairs, or across the street where I hid behind the imposing Methodist church. Once their words concerned my friend Beverly Samm, who lived a block away. Beverly had spoken, or not spoken, to Bess the day before. After an evening's brooding, she was ready to do battle with Beverly, her mother, her father and her grandmother. Somehow that was smoothed over but after that I always went down the street, rather than Beverly coming up the street, to play.

This incident, though hardly memorable, was a good indicator of Bess's profound ability to get her feelings hurt. I learned to walk on eggs those years. The sadness is that this behavior became so ingrained that I was willing to be the resident egg-walker for far too long with far too many. Thus are our lessons poorly learned.

Having been trained to be a good girl, it seldom occurred to me to buck either the system or Bess. When things got rough, I ran, when the waters looked calm, I had my egg-walkers ready, just in case. Every weekend, Bess rode the B&O Railroad back to the environs of Baltimore to see her daughter Gloria. Gloria, five years older than I, lived with another sister, Maude. This suited both Bess and Gloria. Decades later, Gloria in a rare moment of candor, spoke of her years with Tia Maude as the happiest of her life. Lucky Gloria!

Maudie, the baby of the family, was fun and funny. The "tia" was the one Spanish word Gloria retained from a brief babyhood with her Papa Blasini in Puerto Rico. Bess had returned to mother and country when baby Gloria was about three. A handsome man, Papa Blasini was as quick with his fists as Bess was with her anger. Nice Catholic girls did not leave their husbands, and Bess must have felt somewhat like Hester Prynne of "The Scarlet Letter." Mother Walter, an abandoned woman, was always quick with the "I told you so's." Bess's baggage was heavy and there were no little wheels to help her pull it from one day to another.

Although unaware of it at the time, Bess and Betty shared a cautious relationship. I knew that my mother disliked Bess and Bess returned that sentiment, twofold. I learned never to speak of my mother. I became a master (or would it be a mistress?) of avoidance. Don't talk about "it" and "it" will go away. Keeping the peace often carries a price tag that can bankrupt the keeper.

Never directly unpleasant to me, neither was Bess ever more than vaguely congenial. Hugging was not encouraged in the Walter tribe, or many other tribes of the time. We circled a lot, chose our words carefully and became adherents to the credo of surface politeness. As I grew upwards to ten, I longed for the Friday afternoons that would see Bess board the trolley for Baltimore. Of course, I stood at the station waving and smiling. By Sunday evening, after my father and I had done the movie scene and returned to popcorn, listening to Jack Benny on the radio and bringing Poochie up from the basement, a sense of dread would begin to descend. Monday morning loomed and the return train/trolley was always on time.

When my mother gave up on Lake Placid fresh air and returned home, there was a welcome party with Bess, the cook, my father, the angry host, Betty the younger, befuddled, and Betty the elder, crying. My mother ran upstairs. I followed and listened to how Bess had insulted her, had taken over her home, her daughter and "This was no longer to be." Whom to believe? Now I know the truth was halfway between the two opposing forces. Bess left the next morning in the train/trolley with no return ticket. My mother went by automobile to Baltimore to stay with her sister Ellen. My father and I stayed in the big house with no keeper or caregiver. I did not know that decisions about my future were in the works. The Hannah More Academy, oldest Episcopal school in the United States, was soon to be my new home. I did not see Bess again after I graduated. Today, I regret that. She deserved better. Like most of us, she did the best she could with the cards the croupier had dealt.

HANNAH MORE--BEHIND THE LYNCH GATE: 1944-1949

When my mother returned from Lake Placid, discouraged, depressed and disillusioned about the fact that there was no cure, doctors conferred and confirmed the obvious. My remaining in the house was not an option. The decision to send me to the Hannah More Academy in Reisterstown, Maryland was the solution. There were any number of "girl" schools in the area. All in all, this was the best solution.

Anger was my response. Although the feeling was disguised behind the overt reaction of homesickness and free-falling tears, I felt adrift in a sea of rules and strict regulations. Placed initially in grade nine, it was quickly determined that I needed grade eight. Public schools at that time did not include grade eight. Middle school was still a spark in the eyes of educational experts. Not, however, to the ladies at Hannah More.

My rebellion took the form of doing little, if any, work. I read countless books during the required study hall hours. I can still smell the room that housed the desks affixed to the floor. The proctor sat on a platform raised to a level above the study hall. Anything that had to do with reading or writing, I loved. As far as arithmetic was concerned, I did countless summers of summer school. Numbers eluded me; words enthralled.

My lifelong friend, Mary Chapman, adopted me. Also an only child, she took over the mothering role, cajoled me out of tears and into laughter and taught me the meaning of loyalty. She always ranked first in our class of seventeen girls but never judged or condemned my lackadaisical attitude. She taught me to accept people based on who they were rather than how the world added up their accomplishments, or the lack thereof. Mary had many friends. A born leader, we all expected her to become the first woman President. Instead, she married a Harvard classmate, bore four sons, lived the outwardly envied life in Princeton, New

Jersey and survived some tough times. She could not survive the raging cancer that attacked her at age fifty-five. She was a good woman.

With Mary's help, I slowly accepted, outwardly, the regime of Hannah More. I always seemed to be "in trouble." This must be the primary reason that as a teacher I was always drawn to the students who didn't color inside the lines, who found the school house restrictive, and who showed some spark of who they might later become. I had no particular reason to be a rebel, but I enjoyed the role and lived up to the expectations that part demands.

I spent five years at what we all laughingly referred to as the "academy." Although I never reached scholar status, I did carve out a niche uniquely mine. I found identity, acceptance and, of course, status, in being the "wit." Working hard at this role, I gained my own circle of friends and became the scourge of some of the faculty. In ninth grade, I was "discovered" on stage. Naturally, I was funny. Over the next four years, I did funny both on and off the boards. It worked.

What also worked was the family I was part of. When we graduated in 1949, I left a home with sixteen sisters, a few memorable and influential teachers, and the gift of knowing about surviving in a group. In reality, I did more than survive. I had evolved into a different kind of leader than my friend Mary. More of a "storm the Bastille" catalytic agent, I was to remain forever enshrined in the hearts of my sisters as the rebel without a cause but with a great deal of "spunk." I lost "spunk" as the years progressed but occasionally still feel the stirring of my rebellion. Pity I don't feel it more often.

You can, perhaps, better understand these years with the following pictures of some of the teachers, a few students and two males who stood on the periphery of this circle of females.

Some of the ladies of the faculty remain clear in my memory. After all, they taught us, chaperoned us, nursed us, reprimanded us and, as best they were able, nurtured us. Rather than a group hug, we had a group mom. Since few of them had children of their own, we were their surrogate offspring. Few had ever married. Like priests, they were presumed to be celibate, destined to be always in the company of women, and if they longed for another life, they never dreamed aloud. That also was a sign of the times. Fears were closeted, dreams were for the very young, and as Emily Dickinson once said: "Hope is a thing with feathers that perches in the soul...." Here they are. Although all these photos, if available, would be in black and white, I shall attempt to add color to their negatives.

Aunt Gussie: I never saw A.G. in anything but her starched uniform, her lacy cap that signified she had graduated from the University of Maryland School of Nursing, and her spotlessly white shoes that must have demanded a polish nightly. She was nurse practitioner in residence. Florence Nightingale she wasn't! A gruff, large bosomed woman, her main sidekick was a bird lady by the name of Miss Parrot. My clan of the Academy delighted in stealing past Aunt Gussie's door and sneaking peeks into the forbidden, very small apartment. Miss Parrot, straight out of Tennessee Williams, was sometimes perched on the bed while Gussie was ensconced in her rocking chair telling bawdy jokes. Miss Parrot was aptly named. An unofficial chaperon, she must have been someone's sister, first cousin, or poor relation. She always met trains, took underclass girls on buses and generally was the aide-de-camp for those requiring her services. While Gussie loved to unearth a wrong, Miss Parrot was so fearful of confrontation that she not only overlooked the offense but ran in the opposite direction. She did a lot of running.

Miss Eleanor Lewis: Miss Eleanor had two dresses and one cameo brooch: one black, one brown but cut from the same pattern. The only truly thin person I have ever seen with many chins cascading down her neck, she loved literature, feared students, and cried sporadically. Mostly she teared when we threw snowballs in the room, chortled at Beowulf (the Middle English version!) and laughed out loud when she read "Sonnets from the Portuguese." It is with real shame that I confess to being the ringleader here. She was a woman ill designed for teaching, and she deserved better. Truthfully, to deserve better you have to figure out how to better-up the equation. Miss Eleanor was too fragile for this world. However, I must acknowledge her with somehow imparting much more than I gave her credit for in my sophomore year in college. We used the same text for Brit lit that poor Miss Eleanor had used. Suddenly, I remembered things I thought I had never learned. That was the time I should have penned a note to Eleanor Lewis--yet another delayed good intention, another opportunity put on hold. Many of my missed opportunities were missed because I delayed the moment. I try not to delay moments now. I try to let people know what they mean to me. I try to be honest. Let me assure you, I do not always succeed.

Miss Gale: She couldn't have been more than twenty-two. She had recently graduated from Smith, possibly Radcliffe--one of those sister schools. She taught tenth grade English and fell in love with the seemingly available young minister who lived with his mother and to the best of my knowledge, never married. He taught a Wednesday required religion class and officiated at our Sunday services. We loved watching the progress of this in-house boy/girl scenario. All of us giggled and probably wished we could be living her dream. She tried hard, but unsuccessfully, to capture his heart. I doubt that he had one. When I was a senior, the two of us went to the old Ford's Theater to see some play about the Browning's. (What else?) We first went to a great restaurant, Marconi's; I was sixteen, she was probably twenty-four. Certainly I have forgotten what we had to eat but I do have a vivid memory of what we had to drink. Lots of red wine, (age not being a factor in those days). We both had far too much vino and stumbled into the Browning saga where we proceeded to laugh inappropriately at declarations of love everlasting and really hooted when the nutty father terrorized the wheelchair-bound Elizabeth Barrett. Wonderful. "What fools we mortals be," as the bard so cleverly pointed out. I have no idea what happened to Miss Gale. When I returned after my freshman year at Western Maryland, she was no longer there. My hope is that she found someone with a heart.

Mrs. McCormick: Two of her daughters attended Hannah's school. She was the bookkeeper, sender of all bills, and I'm sure wrote lovely notes to creditors. They all resided on Long Island. The Mr. was never mentioned. I think, like the father in the "Glass Menagerie," he, too "fell in love with long distance." The Mrs. was a tough broad. It took some years before I realized that under her phony accent she had what we used to call "spirit." Her hair was closely clipped. She wore closely clipped suits with white bow blouses and cut through the crap with precision and, naturally, clipped speech. Not what could ever be called warm and friendly, she helped to give us something much more important. It was "class." Mrs. Mac said "If you don't have it; learn it." I've always maintained that "you can't buy me love"...or class. She didn't sell us class, she exuded it. Probably some of us picked up on the concept and refigured it to our own personalities. She was a worldly and stabilizing influence for many of us. But it was her toughness I most admired. Unfortunately, I was an inept pupil in that department.

Ferguson: Ran the dining room and even had a song dedicated to him. The tune went along these lines: "When Ferguson brings the ice cream in..." This was routinely warbled every Thursday night when icy slabs of vanilla ice cream with a droplet of chocolate syrup was the dessert of the week. Ferguson always led the procession. Crisp, white coat, perfect manners and a kind heart endeared him to all the girls. He was "colored" as we said back in those long-ago times. He was also my friend. When I wearied of study hall, I would always devise some way to slip out and find Ferguson setting tables, filling water glasses and generally commanding the kitchen troops. He was never too busy to talk. He, too, loved to read, so that became our initial common bond. By the time I graduated, we both cherished our chats. I learned far more from Ferguson than I ever did conjugating Latin verbs.

The Hart sisters: The Hart "girls" as we called them were obviously sisters, and were always together. It was rumored they were vampires, but neither had the lean and hungry look required for blood sucking. They had inherited an enormous, dark and eerie house on the main street in Reisterstown, fit for vampires and thus a perfect setting for Gothic horror tales. One Hart taught piano; the other taught me to despise math in any variety: numbers, lines, angles, percentages, whatever. I particularly disliked the decimal point, always managing to put it in the wrong place. The Hart who played piano had large thumbs, perhaps reinforced by too much practicing on the family keyboard. I considered the Hart who specialized in math, mean-spirited. This view may have been strengthened by my loathing of the subject and hence despising the messenger.

Mary Baldwin: The Baldwin name is well known in the state of Maryland. One side of the family is very rich, the other side very poor. Mary belonged to the poor but very proud side. A tiny girl who grew into a tiny woman, she was very bright, looked to be a member of the starving class, and was my dear friend for our years together. Mary displayed nervous symptoms that I am convinced was a product of inbreeding in the Baldwin clan. Her father dressed like Edgar Allen Poe: long black cape, white shirt, and a permanent melancholic expression that allowed him entrance to the Poe room at the Enoch Pratt Library without benefit of membership. Frightened ticket takers merely assumed they were witnesses to the ghost of Poe. During our tenure at Hannah More, he published a book on the greatness of Poe. It vanished from the shelves soon after publication.

Mary's grandfather was the only southern gentleman I have ever known. Often we visited his enormous, decaying home named Bunker Hill near Millersville, Maryland. He truly looked like Mark Twain, but much older--very old through the eyes of a fourteen-year-old. Slave quarters still stood on the property. He retained a black man and woman who cleaned, cooked and butlered for him. Bunker Hill was always cool, even on the hottest day. Books abounded. I got a tiny glimpse of a way of life I have never seen again. The family retainers, the faded elegance, the portraits of the Baldwin's predating the real Bunker Hill times. Mary had her own horse stabled at the Academy. However, she did not have a winter coat. One Sunday, my father appeared with a heavy, dark red coat with a tiny furry collar for Mary. He handled the giving of the coat in such a way that one would have thought she needed to take it merely to humor him. Mary, for once, did not cry. Years later, she told me that was the most wonderful gift she ever received. I learned many valuable lessons about the frailness of the aristocracy from Mary Baldwin. However, it was my father who taught me the real joy of giving.

Mrs. Bromfield: I adored Mrs. B., as she was called. A divorced woman (not lady) she had wonderfully dyed red hair, high heels that were far removed from the sensible oxfords worn by the maiden ladies, and greatest of all dividends, she was my English teacher in eighth and ninth grades. I guess she was instrumental in sparking my love of written and spoken words, in encouraging me to go forth with "gusto" and hugging me...a lot. Every Friday, Mrs. B. left for parts unknown and returned late on Sunday evening. When she went up the stairs to pack some of her outfits (none were either black nor brown--the standard issue for the other ladies), she sang routinely, "On the road to Mandalay...where the flyin' fishes play." She actually sang quite well and with such verve that I was spellbound. Also, she did some trilling on the word Mandalay, something that sounded like man/da/lay/hey,hey. She transmitted her passion for life, for learning and for an indefinable something that I didn't realize at the time was courage. Decades later, I saw her at Center Stage where I had taken a group to see "Long Day's Journey into Night." Her hair was still red, but her face showed the "ravages" of time and her body was fragile. I went over to her and said "Do you know how much you gave to me?" She answered, "Of course. Do you know what you gave in return?" I shall never forget her answer. It sums up not only what teaching is all about, but what any relationship of worth means. I'm sure Mrs. B. is, as we used to say euphemistically, " long gone." But not really. Part of her is alive within me and in every other girl who heard "man'da'lay/hey/hey" and understood its promise.

MIFFIE: MARY FRANCES GAYLORD

Miffie, a.k.a., Mary Frances Gaylord, was yet another "only." She was more dilatory than I was, an exact opposite in personality from my friend, Mary Chapman. She became my cohort in misdeeds, my friendly competitor, my buddy, and a true friend. Miffie's talent did not extend toward academics. She proclaimed herself an artist and either took on the pre-pre-pre-sixties philosophy, or just truly was one of those rare and genuine free spirits. We liked each other, we enjoyed forbidden smokes in the bathroom, and after lights out we dreamed great dreams together. She would become a renowned artist. I was vague about my destiny. "Writing, maybe?" "Yes," proclaimed Miffie, "and we will share a cold water flat in Greenwich Village." Sure. Miffie became Mary Frances and her quest for the life of the artist actually came true. She lives with paint brushes, the first man she married and two very grown daughters outside of St. Louis. I presume the daughters have long since flown from the sanctuary. Miffie was real people.

I'm sure she still is real people. After graduation, my father and I visited the Gaylord's in Richmond, Virginia where they had lived for generations. With a name like Gaylord, the south would have to be home. Miffie's mother, a truly beautiful woman, was as gracious as her father was withdrawn and seemingly weighed down with sadness. Even at seventeen, I must have had some insight into the human psyche. About a month after our visit, he shot himself in the bathroom. I wrote to Miffie, but she did not respond for several years. I wondered then, as I wonder now, if people who see the gun or the pills as the only alternative ever really consider the aftershocks and the anger that is their legacy. I exclude from this puzzlement people who are terminally ill and choose to leave their existence with dignity while maintaining control over their own life. Miffie was ravaged by the aftermath of her father's death for years. She stopped being Miffie then and became Mary Frances.

After Mary Chapman's death, I received a telephone message from Mary Frances. I responded immediately. She was leaving for Greece the next day to conduct a painting workshop for college art students. I asked her if they spoke English. Her reply, "Ah, who cares. We'll talk with the brush." She had not changed.

It had been forty-five years since we had spoken. Death tends to be a reconnector. We proclaimed our need to see each other. Could we meet halfway? How about New York City? She had this to do, I had that. This and that's have slowed the process. Likely, we will never manage halfway. It's been almost fifty years now. Miffie never returned to any of the reunions. As she said, "You and Mary were the only people I liked. Why would I want to see those nasty girls who are nastier old women now?" Maybe when we acknowledge our fiftieth in 1999, she will come. Somehow, I doubt that! We'll have to work harder on halfway. If we ever do, I will still call her "Miffie."

HANNAH MORE: 25TH REUNION

On a poetically perfect June day in 1974, twelve of the seventeen girls who graduated in the Hannah More Academy class of 1949 returned to acknowledge the irrefutable fact that twenty-five years had passed. The girl/children we had left behind after we "pomped and circumstanced" ourselves out of the matriarchal society that had helped form us were no longer in the company of women who had taught us, nurtured us as best they could, and impressed upon us that we were Hannah More girls: "Handmaidens of the Lord; polished corners of the temple." The signet rings we each wore on graduation day confirmed that ideology. The angel embedded in the gold signet ring reminded us that we were guarded--if not touched--by an angel. Over the next twenty-five years, many of us discovered otherwise.

Our coming together coincided, ironically and somewhat sadly, with the coming apart of Hannah More, the oldest girl's Episcopal school in the United States. Books no longer balanced, teachers demanded more money, girls showed the effects of the 1960s; all those things conspired to bring the rage of the sixties into the once sanctified bastion of civility. Times they were a changing.

And we had changed. Married, with children; divorced, with children. The twelve returnees had passed the landmark of 40. A few had, as we used to say, "married well." That translated into the fact that careers were not part of the well-married package. The majority of those twelve women were products of one of the sister college up north. Wellesley, Smith, Radcliffe were all well represented. One of us, a seemingly unlikely candidate, had become a doctor. One a successful architect, another lawyered in a fancy New York firm. Another had recently married a widowed Methodist minister and busied herself with the church organ, her year-old baby, and the husband's adolescent children that he and the deceased wife had together. Margaret, the new bride/mother, was aglow. Spinsterhood had been averted. The price must have been high since ten years later, the not-so-new bride slit her wrists in the parsonage inAnnapolis.

But on that glorious day in June we toured the school, revisited our rooms, shrugged at the dreariness of the study hall, walked to the stables that had housed the horses we all rode, and tried with varying degrees of success to slip back into the sense of familiarity we had enjoyed, or tolerated, or at least known so many years ago. Most of us had become boarding sisters around age twelve. We had studied together, played field hockey, had that strange female equivalent to the school John Knowles immortalized in "A Separate Peace." Our discussions of sex were so permeated with myth and misinformation it is astonishing that, to the best of my knowledge, none of us became great with child during our freshmen year--even at Smith, Radcliffe or Wellesley. Without any male influence, much less dominance, we closely resembled novice nuns. The only difference: None of us wished to be wedded to Christ.

But all the returnees had, indeed, wedded, to varying degrees of success. Actually, it was not until another fifteen years had passed that I found out some of the truths behind the 25th reunion unified front of "wonderful, wonderfuls." Everything seemed to simmer down or turn up to that credo. Everything—in all our lives—was just grand. None of us dared admit that our "handmaidening" was turning out poorly or that the corners of our temples were crumbling.

Few of us had stayed in touch. Obviously, the sisterhood had not been as strong as we thought. Miffie was notable by her absence. One of the seventeen had died, two had left for parts unknown; correspondence had been stamped "return to sender." The other missing-in-action of the 25th had simply not responded.

We all tried to reconnect with varying degrees of success. It was our communal refusal to break through the guarded niceties of cocktail conversation that seemed to stymie us. We were all stuck, still, at seventeen. Too much time had gone by, too little contact, and a desire to impress each other with either our worldly goods, our perfect families, or our grandiose careers.

Probably what we all took away, after the laughter of the moment, the distilled memories of the past, and the avoidance of any real revelations about our present, is the realization that families, like plants, need nurturing. We simply had not tended to watering the family tree.

Later, we would. After age fifty, we all realized we needed that album of pictures from the past. We were able to provide each other with help in turning the pages and remarking on the faded, but still visible, prints. We were, indeed, family.

WESTERN MARYLAND COLLEGE: 1949-1953

Like a profusion of other small colleges, Western Maryland College at a time before Eisenhower became President, was ideally situated. Rolling hills, sturdy brick buildings, an enormous edifice aptly named Alumni Hall where plays were performed, compulsory Sunday evening chapel was cut by countless students like myself, and visiting speakers either enthralled or sedated. Life was very different. One was supposed to check in at 10 o'clock on Friday and no later than 11 o'clock on Saturday. Mrs. Veal was our checker-inner at Blanche Ward Hall where I bunked with my long-time friend Barbara Lambert for three years. Mrs. Veal was a sweet old lady whose eyesight was failing and her hearing impaired. Now I wonder if she was perhaps the kind of lady who chose not to see and merely pretended not to hear. Probably.

My first year was spent off campus at an old house called Cassell Hall. The Dean of Women, Helen Howery, lived there with her very aged and extremely unpleasant mother. Sixteen girls walked up the hill to the main campus and back down for dinners with the Dean and her mother. I acclimated slowly to life with both boys and girls. Given all my experience of living with females, I was voted president of Cassell Hall. This gained me entry into various campus organizations that were supposed to fight for student rights, or whatever. I recall no fighting for rights but a great deal of drinking coffee in the Student Union.

Televisions were only owned by the very wealthy. We were, therefore, removed from the world outside. Another womb, but this time with less rules and reasonable restrictions. I enjoyed, once again, living in a house with so many sisters. Two of my first friends at Cassell Hall were Sally Fisher and Barbara Lambert. In the way of all circular ironies, they are both in the Memory Picture class I now teach at Notre Dame College.

Sally, the perennial May Queen, was very pretty, always smiling, and seemingly without doubts or worry. The boys clamored after her. She was envied by many girls, but never seemed impressed by her own aura or enthralled by the contingent of unbearded fresh-faced freshmen boys who rang the bell at Cassell Hall or called begging for her to twirl around the dance floor with them. All she wanted was a degree in Home Economics, a loving husband akin to the ones we saw in the celluloid fantasies that played at the local movie house, many rosy-cheeked children and perhaps a picket fence to protect this vision from unseen forces that might dare to intrude into this perfect world. Sally got her many children; their father, however, was not destined to sit at the head of the table smiling benevolently as he sliced the Sunday chicken. Her life collided with the dream. For my class she wrote a short piece on the death of her son Bill, an example of what can happen along the route. Sally not only survived; she is a woman now sixty-five who radiates the inner Sally. The outer Sally has faded and been replaced with a far different and far more beautiful person.

Barbara came from a childhood of security and love, isolated from the rest of Maryland in a place called Oakland. Remote, bitterly cold in the winter, her memory of childhood was reflected in a piece she wrote called "Hoar Frost." It is not the beauty of the writing that is notable; it is rather the friendship of almost fifty years we have maintained with one another. We knew each other in those years, and like each other now. Perhaps that is the key to unraveling one of the many riddles of the universe!

I encountered a few great teachers at Western Maryland. Esther Smith was that one teacher you always remember. I've been lucky that there were four or five teachers who truly touched my life. No one ever equaled Esther. I speak not just for myself but for countless WMC students who passed through her studio, performed on stage for her and counted her as a true friend.

Esther Smith was, first and foremost, a lady. Coming from Georgia, neither she nor her sister Lillian ever married. Lillian died when she was in her sixties, but not before writing several books. The one that became a classic, and the first to focus on a black/white love affair was *Strange Fruit*. This was back in the Jim Crow era, long before Martin Luther King raised our universal consciences, and when Afro-Americans were referred to as "Colored" or "Niggers," depending on which part of the country one hailed from. Esther had a beautiful speaking voice, called most of us "Honey" and was the quintessential "Steel Magnolia." What did she do that was so unusual?

She imbued us with a sense of self-discipline, a respect for the roles we played, a love of theater, the ability to learn more about ourselves, and about those far different from who or what we were, and in some mysterious manner, gave many of us a lifelong connection to the spirit she dared to show us. She so willingly gave of herself that we went the step, the yard, or even the mile beyond what we suspected we were capable of achieving. Maybe she gave us courage. Maybe she set an example that somehow we wanted to emulate. Certainly, I never achieved her heights, but I do believe that some of her ability to love her students, to truly care about what happened to them, to let them know that they could always go to her and she would listen, rubbed off on many of us. I would like to believe that she lives today in the spirit of the countless students who became teachers, doctors, lawyers and those who just, became.

Esther is a difficult person to write about, even four decades later, because she was a most "beloved" person. Truly, I know of no one who did not admire, love and respect her ability as a teacher, her genius as a director and her strength as a human being.

I must not recreate this very real woman in the mold of a saint. She deserves better. In imbuing her with "ability, genius, strength," do I place her on a pedestal that can only topple? I simply did not know the dark side of Esther. I doubt that any of her students did. I can guarantee you that her sister and her intimate friends would draw another aspect of this woman who

49

would scoff at elevation to the divine. Deification is as dangerous to the sainted as it is to the deifier. No one should ever be burdened with sainthood.

There is one "Estherism" that we all remember and occasionally fall back on when recalling Esther. When she prepared us for whatever role we were assuming on the stage of Alumni Hall, she would say: "When you speak, speak to that lump of dignity at the very top of your head." We would speak. Then, she would say, softly, "Now, do it again." Although I have never qualified as dignified, I know that I, too, have that "lump of dignity." She was the first person to make me aware of its existence. I wish I had understood the implications at that time.

Esther died early in 1996. She was ninety-three years old but reportedly retained her spirit until the end. A memorial service was held for her one Sunday afternoon in early September at Western Maryland College. Students who ranged in age from seventy to thirty-five came to pay tribute to a woman whose influence continues in our lives. This was her final memorial.

I loved the English classes, gave up any vague idea of becoming a doctor after the first dissection of a frog, weathered history with Dr. Whitfield, conned my way through while managing never to gaze at the stars through a telescope, and found my place on the stage under the direction of Miss Esther. "The smell of the greasepaint, the roar of the crowd" did it for me. Oddly enough, it still does today.

A lazy student except in the areas I loved, I graduated with a B.A. in 1953. I knew I would never teach. Too boring. The majority of students who graduated with me had majored in education and minored in marriage. Some had already found their one-and-only. More importantly, they were prepared to earn a living. I knew I had to do something. So, I went to Columbia University to get yet another degree. This was not due to any great desire on my part to access knowledge or worship at the throne of renowned teachers. New York sounded exciting, the possibilities seemed endless, the subways were still safe, and I was twenty-one years old.

WESTERN MARYLAND COLLEGE: 40TH REUNION

The roads leading back to Westminster, Maryland are sleeker than they were forty years ago. The automobile we traveled in was as slick as the new superhighway. Encased in steel, we were protected from any intrusive bump, noise or climatic disturbance by the expertise of the engineers at BMW. The three of us were returning with varying degrees of reluctance to the fortieth reunion of the Western Maryland class of 1953.

Barbara, Bill and I were longtime friends returning to observe and be observed, to assess in some corner of our subconscious how we compared to our fellow graduates, to sift through old memories and now unknown lives to see how we compared. This was not about dressing for or acting out "Success." Those games belong to twentieth reunions. Maybe this drive back into Western Maryland country was about courage. Neither admirable nor spectacular courage, just a little dab of pluck, a touch of chutzpah, and a dash of stage presence--the kind required to attend a cocktail party without alcohol, a dinner without endearing companions or an office Christmas party without a clearly marked exit.   As we drove into the parking lot of the bleak little roadside bistro, Barbara's first words to me were "Give it a chance." My response was "Tacky place." Bill's only comment was "You got that right." We went in.

I knew we were in for it when we signed our now names and were immediately handed a "Hi, I'm..." badge. Our yearbook picture from forty years ago stared back encased under plastic. Was that page-boy'd, bright-eyed girl really me? Had I ever been that young? Would I pin this identifier on my sixty-year-old bosom so long forgotten classmates could know "who is" by checking with the picture of "who was"? Barbara followed orders; I merely slipped the past into the present leather handbag.

"Hey, Betty. How ya doin'?" My god, it's Nell. The voice seems unchanged, the vigor undeniable. The "Let's have a party" punch was still intact. "Fine." Now, there's a clever retort. Safe, noncommittal, this frequent flyer four-letter-word is a social passport into situations where talk of the weather is only surpassed by chatter about incidents long forgotten...or those that should be. Fine, we were all fine, and fine we would all remain.

"Hey, it's Betty, right? Where's your badge? I'm Roland. Remember?" Yes, I remember Roland. Roland has, like most of us, greyed up, bellied up, and actually come up from North Carolina with Mrs. Roland, class of '54. Western Maryland couples of 1950s tended to meet and mate on the rolling hills that surrounded our Methodist enclave. Most are still married to the first person chosen for lifetime vows. "I'm fine, Roland. And you?" "Great." Great always sounds heartier, more positive, more together than "fine." I decided to switch to "great."

I saw Sally. We smiled ruefully at each other. We did not need to look at badges since neither of us had badged. Dismissing both great and fine, we talked briefly and said prophetically, "We must do something about getting together." We had no way of knowing that it would be three years before we did. I was to begin a writing of memories class at the local college. Sally, never a writer, joined the class and became a chronicler of her story. She proved to be remarkable in her ability to touch her listeners.

"Hi Bet. How's tricks?" Neither fine nor great would do for this one. "Business has been off since Hutzler's tea room closed." Silence. Delayed yucks, and one of those "You haven't changed a bit" numbers. Right. Elmer, aptly named, insists I sit between him and Jayne. This invite brought the first prevarication of the noon hour. "Sorry, I promised Janet I'd play catch-up with her." It seemed to work.

Ah, I wondered if he'd be here. And here he is. Forty years later, he has neither grayed nor bellied. He has, however, not withstood all the ravages of time. The face is lined, the hair noticeably thin, but the presence is still pungent with a certain aura. I think it used to be called sex appeal. "Hello, Betty. This is the first one of these things I've come to. I never felt the need before this one. How about you?" What about me? One's needs at sixty can be scary. What is it we're looking for? Validation, forgiveness, someone to tell us we haven't changed? Someone to let us believe for a moment we've changed for the better? Jay, a fellow English major, would-be actor and former "first love" had become a most successful lawyer. "Oh, I'm great." Finally, a "great" opportunity. We cocktail prattled, touched upon grown children and baby grandchildren, and assiduously avoided any mention of marriages and subsequent divorces. We were so gracious, so convivial and so inconsequential. Naturally "doing lunch" was mentioned. We turned away from each other. We both knew there would be no chicken salad in our future.

"Theda. How's it going?" Beth seemed unscathed. She had always called me Theda, as in Theda Bara, the vamp of the silent films. When talkies came in, Theda went out. I had forgotten that nickname gleaned in drama classes. "I'm still upright." Beth and I are always crossing carts at the Super Fresh. Once referred to as "baby" because she was a full year younger than the rest of us, the baby had toughened. Her little boat had survived some major storms and she had handled them with something I had never quite gotten a handle on: grace under pressure. "You know, I swore I wouldn't come to this. What the hell are we doing here, Theda?" "Damn if I know." Two philosophers finally getting the answer? It was time to eat.

Before a buffet of canned green beans, an unapproachable macaroni concoction and overcooked everything, Ashley Collins, our very long-ago class president, decided to do cute. Recognitions and nods for remembered triumphs seemed to be in order. Actually, they were very out-of-order, but Ashley prevailed. I was seated next to Beth, formerly Witzke (the East Baltimore Funeral Home barons) when Nancy, once Kroll, looking preserved in time, was called to the front line. Her pageboy hair was the same, her outfit reminiscent of what *Seventeen Magazine* suggested for college girls of the 1950's, but her approach to the front was sadly slow. Maybe it was the Nike tennis shoes on her tiny feet that proclaimed that things are never quite what they seem. Ashley presented her with the yellowed, preserved-in-plastic college newspaper with her long-ago picture emblazoned on the front page. "Nancy Kroll voted The Most Beautiful. Will Be May Queen for Class of 1953." There it was; here she is. The paper was given to the queen. She walked painfully back to her table. Radiant with memory, she carried the past with reverence. I turned to Beth. "Jesus...What happened?" "She had a breakdown five years ago. Her husband died. Now she lives with her parents. They cope." I turned away. It was too painful to watch.

We ate, we chatted, we took the required class picture. Smile? You're forty years older. A contingent of Blanche Ward Dorm women suggested dinner. If I knew I would never do chicken salad with an almost forgotten beau, I was absolutely certain I would forego fish-of-the-day with these once rollicking girls. Truth of the matter, so would those women who no longer rollicked.

So, why did we all return? Perhaps curiosity or some distorted sense of duty. Perhaps, a need to acknowledge how far we had all come. It took me a long time to shed the Nancy Kroll of 1993. Having taught one of her daughters, my sadness intensified. But it was not all sadness. Some brief encounters with classmates four decades older had shown me, once again, that Thomas Wolfe was right. "You Can't Go Home Again." Maybe some of us just wanted to try.

NEW YORK, NEW YORK: 1953-1956

My New York adventure began with getting off the subway at 125th Street in Harlem instead of 125th Street and Riverside Drive. It was a very warm day in late June. Harlem, all current realities, myths, and homicide stats aside, was an enclave just like Riverside Park that rose above it. In fact, one could walk up a few hundred steep steps to get to the upper realms of Columbia from the lower realms of Harlem. After asking numerous people, none of whom had white faces, how to get to my destination, one finally directed me to a cab. He must have known that I was destined to be subway challenged. I finally arrived.

Yet another dorm. Mercifully, I had a small sitting room, probably designed for studying rather than entertaining, and a bedroom. I was three weeks from Western Maryland College and light years from anything I had known before.

Registered for a class in journalism at the famous school that is part of the University, I also signed on for an acting class at the Teacher's College. I believed I was "finding myself." Without any discernible goal, driving ambition or even vague notions of how to fashion a future, what I did discover was a for-real love. Six weeks is the ideal time span for a first love. Like the summer romance, both parties know the end is in sight. The ship will eventually dock, the cruise will be over and the revelers will depart for hometowns far from dockside.

David was thirty years old, an actor, a teacher outside of Chicago, and as much as I despise this term "we fell in love," this was real, not a celluloid fantasy, a let's pretend so we aren't dateless on the weekend, or an adolescent hormonal surge that blazes and quickly dies due to wax that burns too quickly.

Containing all the trappings of every cliché-ridden Grade B movie ever produced, I would like to believe we brought more to this still lovely memory than the script suggested. When the summer session was over, I returned to Glen Burnie for a brief visit. David returned to his wife of twelve years, his daughter whose age coincided with the length of the marriage, and continued success as a Chicago-based actor. Months later, I received a letter. Unhappy, wanting to break the ties that bound, David suggested we meet at Christmas to regroup, maybe rearrange, maybe change the script. Somehow I had the courage not to answer. I would like to believe that this decision was evidence of character, not the beginning of cowardice.

Malingering along in courses designed to warrant Master of Fine Arts, I busied myself with some course work, some work-work as a receptionist in the Fine Arts Department and a lot of playing in the Lion's Den. This was the meet-to-eat bistro bully-up-for-beer Student Union where everyone went to eat, drink, meet, and because we were graduate students, discuss the meaning of life and the eternal riddle of the universe. On one of my scouting expeditions, I drank a few beers with a Ph.D. candidate by the name of Dean Miller. We laughed, a lot. Both of us had learned early that wit was the way to go. We met more, laughed more and decided we liked each other. The summer of 1954, I was employed at Summer Theater in Vermont. Having for some obscure reason signed on as a costumer, it did not take more than one day for the leaders to learn that I could not sew. Thereafter, I collected props, learned a great deal about theater, had some very small parts, and loved every minute of this experience. My new beau came for a visit for a few days. It crossed my mind that away from the Lion's Den, this relationship seemed rocky. Naturally, I did not allow this fleeting thought to deter our plans for blessed matrimony.

On January 23, 1956, we were married in the living room of my home in Glen Burnie. My father, remarried in mid-October to a grand and gracious lady by the name of Catherine Shipley, seemed a little unsettled by this very tall, very skinny, very young, and very poor young doctoral candidate. I had just turned twenty-three, and knew all my worries were over. Finally, a Mrs., beringed and renamed, I set off with my new mate into the snowstorms that led to Rock Island, Illinois. And thus we began.

MARY HAYDEN: WHAT THE YEARS GAVE US

I have two friends from childhood, if one can consider age eleven still in the realm of that particular "hood" of those who have weathered the journey with me. Both entered my life during those few years before the onset of puberty and the offset of a belief that all stories end happily, all marriages are made in heaven and that all good girls get their just rewards. Both, oddly enough, are named Mary and share the fact that the first initial of their married names begins with "H." They share other similarities far more significant than a name and an initial. Although they have never met, they are cut from the same kind of cloth. They are what used to be referred to as "strong women," which translated into the fact that when life dealt them harsh blows (and, in both cases, it certainly did), they responded with a perceptible strengthening of their respective backbones, a determination to do whatever had to be done to maintain some sense of balance in a world gone awry, and gave new meaning to a concept I never quite achieved: grace under pressure. In other words, they are women to be admired. Admirable women frequently are not particularly lovable women since they tend to trip over their own nobility. Neither of these Mary's ever tripped; in fact, "nobility" was never a factor, and they have both contributed to my life in ways that make each of them especially dear to me.

One of the Mary's greeted me on my first day at the Hannah More Academy. Like myself, she was an only child. Unlike myself, she had a well-developed sense of who she was, of what this boarding school business was all about, plus a contagiously friendly demeanor that I immediately latched onto. She was as relentless in her determination that I would *not* continue to be miserable, as I was that I would suck all the marrow out of my misery that my unleavened anger and palpable homesickness would allow. As I recall, I ran a full year fueled by unrelenting misery. Eventually that tank dried up. By twelve, misery had grown somewhat boring and I found that I could make more friends by making them laugh than having them watch me cry. I wasn't consistently voted "wittiest" for nothing! Sarcasm became an identifier, and in the world of the unidentified, we grab on to the life preserver that keeps us afloat with the least amount of effort.

For those five years at this small and academically prestigious Episcopal girls' school, I managed to avoid the academics except for English with grim determination. While Mary's natural intellect thrived, my laziness flourished, and in a class of seventeen, Mary ranked first and I ranked sixteenth. Our equally disinterested but highly gifted artist friend Miffie Gaylord ranked seventeenth. Mary and I have often said, "Wonder whatever happened to Miffie." Whatever did, I know that being seventeenth did not color her life.

In those five years at Hannah More, this small band of girls and equally small band of mostly live-in instructors were, indeed, family. Mary first took me under her wing, then as I slowly gave up the fight to being voted "most miserable," she took me into her heart and became that universal constant all adolescent girls most long for: the best friend. Only in response to the demanding needs of adolescence do we harken to that inner voice that tells us there "must be a best." Later, if we are fortunate, we realize that each friend offers us what is "best" in them, and we respond in kind. If we are truly blessed, we also recognize and accept the flip side of that "best" and cherish that person because they are real, because their flaws humanize them and because we accept each other for what we are, not for what others might want us to be.

From 1944 to 1949, not only Mary but also her parents became a positive factor in my life. My mother at home coughed angrily at her enemy, tuberculosis. Her arsenal of weapons was limited to Pall Mall cigarettes and Hershey Bars with Almonds. Since there were no power drugs that would feed into the canon of defense, she never tried to outwit her adversary, merely to defy him. Juxtaposed to this picture was a home in Mercersburg, PA, where Mary returned each summer. Her father, a Harry Trumanesque gentleman, taught history at the Mercersburg Academy. Her mother, a woman who could have organized the first wagon train west and successfully defied any white or red man who tried to stop her, was gifted with a kind heart coupled with a pragmatic view of the human condition. Their home was a monument to what two frugal, determined, hard-working people could accomplish. It contained furniture collected at auctions beautiful beyond belief, pictures that looked as if they belonged in a museum, and china and silverware that spoke of a graciousness one seldom sees today. Mary has much, if not all of this, in her home in New Jersey. Whenever I see these pieces, I am taken back to a time fifty years ago when the kindness of these dear people touched my heart and enriched my life.

Finally, the coughing stopped. The enemy planted his flag of death in the summer between my junior and senior year. Mary's parents, somehow, knew what to do. My father and I were gathered up by Mary's northward-ho mother and taken to Wells Beach, Maine. There, in a house literally owned by Mary's mother, literally by the ocean, the healing began. Mary and I took to the wonderfully isolated beach where we proceeded to read aloud *The Love Song of J. Arthur Prufrock*. Then, as now, when I read the following lines, I cry:

No! I am not Prince Hamlet, nor was meant to be;
Am an attendant Lord, one that will do
To swell a progress, start a scene or two
Advise the prince, no doubt, an easy tool
Deferential, glad to be of use
Politic, cautious, and meticulous/
Full of high sentence, but a bit obtuse
At times, indeed, almost ridiculous--
Almost, at times, the Fool

There is a major difference between the then and the now, as indeed there always is. Sitting on the beach at age sixteen, I only loved the way the words seemed to flow plus the fact that I had recently seen some handsome young fellow in a local production of "Hamlet" and thought I was dying of unrequited love. It was such a seductive misery (the fact that I had never met the Hamlet actor fellow did not intrude into what I considered the high drama) that I wept copiously at "Almost, at times, the Fool." At age sixty I no longer weep but certainly get more than dewy-eyed at this passage. In fact, in those intervening years between 16 and 60, I have had so many occasions to think of those lines that I even considered titling my recollections, "Am an attendant Lord." Mercifully, good sense, or good humor prevailed after I realized book browsers might think this a religious tome penned by a disgruntled nun.

My father and I traveled to Wells Beach for several summers and became part of Mary and her mother's generosity of spirit and kindness of heart. College prevailed, marriages began, locations changed, children became, and suddenly...we were thirty. Neither of us was especially adept at putting pen to paper. There was the obligatory Christmas card with the usual catch-up news of how wonderfully life was treating us good girls and how we must "get in touch." Since Ma Bell was not encouraging anyone to "reach out and touch" long distance unless the message dealt with death, divorce or related disasters, our contact lagged. Mary had permanently nested in the Princeton area and I was in the nearby but not so nearly nice area of New Brunswick, New Jersey. There, my husband, the eternal student of Byzantine History and the father of my two sons, was pursuing his doctorate and, as a diversion from the rigors of academia, was tracking another woman.

Once, on a hot July afternoon, I rode over to Princeton, one three-year-old and one nine-month-old in tow to seek solace from Mary. While her three boys and my two either splashed in a pool or dozed in a stroller, we tried to make some kind of sense out of an upside down world in the environs of New Brunswick that was as far removed from Brigadoon as one could imagine. Even with the splashing and squabbling, the tears followed and Prufrock's bewilderment became less poignant in the fact of one's own reality. The words were comforting, the love sustaining, but my wounds were too fresh and too deep for any salve my old friend could offer. The jaws of life suddenly started to nip at my heels. It would be several years down the road before Mary became their prey.

Ultimately, there was a divorce. I moved "back home." It was 1962, when single parenting was akin to scarlet lettering. Hester had nothing on me, at least in my perception of the situation. There was a very occasional missive between Mary and myself. The balm of time did its inevitable work. The "other woman" did not ride off into the sunset with her love-struck married suitor. Instead, she remained married, I remarried, the Byzantine scholar received his doctorate, relocated to a distant upper New York State university and took to wife a woman with a son from her prior marriage. "All's well that ends well?" Not funny, McGee.

Mary and I did not connect again until our twenty-fifth reunion. How, one might ask, could so much time go by without contact? Years ago, I might have tried to answer all questions. Now, I understand that there are no answer books and even if there were, we would not know on what page to find for sure that 2 + 2 always equals 4. When our class of seventeen reconnoitered there were thirteen who returned. One seemed to be missing in marital action somewhere, another chose not to answer the reunion missive, yet another lived too far away, and Miffie, bless her heart, was busy painting yet another picture. She had, it seems, become a well-known and respected artist in St. Louis. So much for being seventeen.

Mary and I stayed up most of the night, along with other drinking buddies, reliving the past, discoloring the present and avoiding the future. In other words, just what one would expect from a group of 42-year-old women, some who had not touched base for twenty-five years. We were all unnaturally happy, healthy, adored our husbands, and had the most remarkable children imaginable, careers that were fulfilling or, if money was not a concern, volunteer work that demonstrated our social consciousness. Add to that the fact that we were Hannah More girls who somehow, over a few nights, turned into forty-two-year-old women living out the ethics taught to us "behind the Lynch Gate." For those unfamiliar with that prepositional phrase it was one impaled (literally) over the entrance to Hannah More. Although I had always fancied myself the actress, later I was to realize that Mary had been far better than I during this encounter. I was not aware that the jaws of life had her marital heels painfully and firmly in tow.

The truth is that I was not aware of much about Mary's life until many years later at a Hannah More election day luncheon in Annapolis, Maryland. Strangely enough, about eight or nine returned, all on time, all older and certainly wiser. Less inclined to do what all of us had been trained to do, we started to speak honestly about some of the "vicissitudes of fortune" and the "ravages of time." (There goes Prince Hamlet speaking about himself. Prufrockian echoes could be heard in much of what was said--or unsaid—at the table.) Mary was there looking as well turned out as always. When I saw her, I teared up. My father was dying, her father had died. Her first marriage was long over; her second marriage a testament to the fact that second chances are there if the right two people do not gamble on unrealistic expectations. My second marriage was over; a fatality of the wrong two people with diametrically different personalities and contrary expectations. The only similarity we shared was a Hamlet-like inability to take direct action. If necessity is the mother of invention, procrastination is the father of despair!

Mary's mother had lived with her until the need of a nursing home ultimately intruded into that arrangement. Mary's grown children were doing well, she had a job gotten through necessity after her divorce and developed through passion over a period of time. She was hale and hearty and we picked up where we had left off years before. As I looked around the luncheon table, I realized how far all of us had traveled and that for many of us the journey was far different than the map we thought we were following. There had been no road signs to warn us of how roads get slippery when wet and someone with a wicked sense of the absurd had hidden all the detour signs. However, we all had avoided any fatal accidents, and so far none of us had been totaled.

Since I gave up on Christmas cards years ago when I found that season of the year to be, for all the usual reasons, one tough sucker to get through, I was surprised to get a green bell or holly leaf (one of those Christmas things) from Mary in March following our Annapolis lunch. I happened to love Christmas cards in March; I did not love the brief message. She had a cancer of the lung; it had been dealt with. She was getting better, although still a little weak. Suddenly, I was eleven again.

Without hesitation, without any mulling over should I or shouldn't I, will she or won't she, I picked up the telephone decades after Ma Bell had encouraged us to touch frequently and often through the high tech convenience of Touch Tones. I touched the information robot lady in Philadelphia, got the number and within seconds the voice connection was there and the time connection reclaimed.

Shortly thereafter, I visited Mary and her husband in Philadelphia. She looked wonderful, was recuperating at a great rate, and we faced each other as though the intervening years had been a whisper in time. My father had died in August of the year before. I was in the process of dealing with some matters that were emotionally wracking. How wonderfully releasing it was to talk to Mary. Time dropped away, the decades faded, and what remained was a basis begun in "childhood," an understanding of who we had been, what we had become and how our parents had colored the parameters of the portrait of what we were at that moment in time. The loneliness of the fiftyish "only" is that there are no siblings to verify the memory, to help expose the negative, or to look through the picture album with you and say, "Do you remember this day?" "Look at how happy he looked there," "See how young she was then." We shared the joy and the pain of opening our albums. After all, we actually knew the people in the pictures.

Shortly after that visit, I returned to the "boards," an unexpected lesson in the fact that not only is it "never too late" but that taking risks is all a part of the journey. I had always, God knows, understood that old saw about "no pain, no gain." Now I realized that "no risk, no hiss" was also true. I discovered that, indeed, no one hissed during the run of this dinner theater musical and that what I had so enjoyed in college (the seduction of the power to make an audience laugh) was still there. Like riding a bike? Well, maybe!

Mary and her husband traveled down from the City of Brotherly Love to show that sisterly love does not always require the yearly Christmas card, that a decade can slip by without any contact, and that long-distance does not mean one is distanced.

Since that time, I have visited Mary twice in her home in New Jersey. The first time, one of the hottest days on record, we sat on a screened-in porch and mulled over the meaning of life and the mystery of the universe, or whatever. I remember saying, between slurps of very iced tea, "What's it all about?" I shall always remember Mary's response, "I don't know, but it's worth the trip."

The next time I visited, Mary's cancer had returned. It was a few days after Christmas and very hot had been replaced, as is the wont of Mother Nature, with very chilly, dark and gloomy. My fellow traveler to New Jersey was a dear and trusted friend. For reasons that defy explanation, I wanted my nearby friend and confidant to meet my longtime Mary. They connected, as I knew they would. Mary's husband coupled with the two of us and we shared one of those brief moments in time that validates what Mary had said on that hot summer evening, "It's worth the trip."

The cancer has, in the way of disease maps that don't show the roadblocks, spread. Mary is, at this moment in time, struggling with the after effects of chemo and the now effects of morphine. No, life is not fair. That's a given. Is it worth the trip? Absolutely. Friends like Mary have shown me that whatever the cost, the trip must be undertaken with understanding that there are no guarantees. The return policy is nonexistent, and the croupier in charge of our communal gambling table cannot always be trusted. I shall always treasure my long ago, afraid to take the trip. We were children together, and part of us always remembers eleven.

I knew when Sharlene and I left Mary and Weld a few days after Christmas of 1992 that I would never see Mary again. Once a month, I called to "check in." Sometimes Mary was in the hospital, occasionally we spoke briefly. In the middle of June, approximately six months after the Christmas visit, I called and Weld told me that Mary's condition was perilous. Did I have any books to send up that he might read aloud to her?

Instead of sending books, I sent my memory of Mary. Her impending death was a catalyst for me to write it down. Within five minutes of talking to Weld, I began my tribute to Mary, my memory of our long association that I hoped included some of my feelings about what our friendship had meant to me. I wrote quickly. Whatever you have read here is what came out. Later, when I attempted to rewrite, delete, add to, I simply could not. This is one memory that could not afford cosmetic surgery!

After sending the Mary piece to Weld, I did not hear anything for about two weeks. One beautiful Sunday afternoon, July 10, I stopped at a convenience store to get some milk. As I got back into the car, I looked up at a perfect sky. I knew immediately that Mary had died. Five minutes later, I picked up my telephone messages. The first one was from Weld stating that, indeed, Mary had died that morning. I called to find out about funeral arrangements and Weld told me how many times he had read my memory to Mary. Even when she could not speak, she would gesture when she wanted to hear certain passages again. Weld had copies made for each of Mary's sons.

67

The Memorial Service was held at a chapel in Princeton where Mary and Weld had been married six years before her death. A brass ensemble played some of her favorite music. A few people spoke. There was no body, no ashes, and the service was according to Mary's wishes. Afterwards, we returned to the beautiful home in Rocky Hill with the magnificent grounds. It was one of those perfect evenings. Neither too hot nor too chilly, Mary must have ordered this as she had requested that everyone who attended the funeral come back for some food and companionship before they headed home. These people had gathered to celebrate a life that although far too short had encompassed the attributes we all strive for: courage, loyalty, steadfastness, love. "Sing No Sad Songs For Me" was the refrain I heard in my mind. Others must have heard it too. A hundred people paid tribute to her life by doing their part to add dignity to her death. I remembered how we had both loved a segment from John Donne. Perhaps it is appropriate to close Mary's chapter by merely stating those few lines:

Each man's death diminishes me
For I am involved in mankind
Therefore, send not to know
For whom the bell tolls:
It tolls for thee.

As it will toll for all of us, never shall I forget Mary or her legacy: "It's worth the trip."

BESSIE MILLER: MORE THAN A MOTHER-IN-LAW

While the Midwest reels from flood devastation during the summer of 1993, I sit in my tiny air-conditioned cocoon reading about what some trauma psychologist deemed the "collective unconscious" of the thousands of displaced farmers and ordinary people who have responded with a kind of inbred courage one seldom sees today. To me, this is best summed up with the words of Joan Crabill, a farming wife, who said, "It's the way I expected it to be. You have to roll with the punches and just go on."

Bessie Miller, Midwest born and bred, long-time inhabitant of Rock Island, Illinois, was, technically, through my marriage to her son, my mother-in-law. During our journey together, the designee of "in-law" was dropped. Instead of being a casualty of the divorce process, Bessie became one of the most important contributors to my life. It was through her example of "rolling with the punches and just going on" that I first learned that courage is not defined by actors playing on the filmed battlefields of World War II. Before Bessie, my vision of "hero" had been steadfastly shaped by John Wayne in "The Shores of Iwo Jima," by Van Johnson in "A Guy Named Joe," by Dana Andrews forever being a prisoner of the Japanese and by a flickering image of Veronica Lake, hand grenade in hand, making the ultimate sacrifice to save the lives of many at the altar of self-destruction. Bessie taught me about private battles that no filmmaker at the time would have been interested in recording. The lesson I learned from her is that courage is a singular affair, a personal battle, and has nothing to do with hand grenades, guns, or surviving the horrors of prison camp. Her prison was diabetes run amok. One leg was amputated, poor circulation being the victor in that battle. Her eyesight slowly waned and finally faded completely. Diabetes won that war. However, Bessie's spirit not only survived; it ultimately will be remembered as the real victor.

I first met Bessie Miller a few days after my marriage to her only son in January of 1955. Leaving the scene of the nuptials (which, counter to the norm of the time, had been performed in the living room of the family homestead), the newly minted "we" began a treacherous trek into a part of the country I had never seen. A massive snowstorm either followed or preceded us over every state between Maryland and Illinois. What awaited us in Rock Island was not only worth the trip, but was the beginning of what I now realize was the first link in my search for someone to help me define the concept of mother. My own mother's illness disallowed both of us access to that vital relationship. Bessie Miller, unknowingly, provided that link.

Bessie, like many women of her generation, was born at the wrong time. Formed and fashioned by the Depression, she never journeyed beyond high school. Instead, her agile mind found an outlet in her nimble fingers. Her innate creativity discovered a conduit in the organ at the local Presbyterian Church and at the sewing machine in her bedroom. Through these two instruments, she helped to define herself and put her signature on that intangible something we all need if the journey is to have any meaning beyond the mundane.

Was she a particularly sensitive organist? Truthfully, I don't know. My musical ear hardly qualifies as finely tuned. I do know she played with joy, loved the sounds she made and passed on organ genes to one of her daughters, a truly accomplished musician. The sewing machine as a creative outlet is a topic I can speak to! Bessie shipped, seemingly without effort, outfits for me that I still remember in detail. How is it possible that more than thirty-five years later, the black suit that would have made Miss Chanel look up from her pattern making, a red dress with a triangular white bib, maternity clothes that defied the usual belly expanders fashionable at that time, and countless other examples of fashionable feathers, still are so vivid in my memory bank? Now I belatedly understand that it was not the cut of the fabric or the beauty of the material but the love that went into the product that still provides the lens through which I can see her creations.

Those clothes were a gift from the heart. They could not be bought and the memory of them cannot be stolen. Bessie provided me with much more than conveyors to a fashion statement. She gave me back myself.

Even before the honeymoon was over in Rock Island, Bessie said to me, "I had two daughters, now I have a third." This should not be taken as a direct quote, but rather as a directly honest statement from a woman incapable of dishonesty. Many newly minted mothers-in-law mouth this sentiment, but never put their metaphoric money where their actual mouths are. Of course, most are never put to the test! The test came for Bessie shortly before the seventh anniversary of our homestead wedding, shortly after the birth of our second son and shortly following the introduction of that mainstay character on the afternoon soaps: the other woman. "The Age of Innocence" drew to a rather thunderous halt. Bessie came to help with the care and tending of the newborn, to grandmother the first-born and to nurture the new mother. Needless to say, she got more than she bargained for. The beginning of the end is always painful. If Bessie was a woman born before her time, I was a thirty-year-old girl/woman ill prepared for this onslaught of reality.

My marriage had been a rather placid one. Fashioned around all the benevolent beliefs of the 1950's, it was destined to wear thin, then down, then out. However, somewhat like a boxer thrown into the ring without benefit of gloves, helmet or tooth protector, I was not quite ready for the knockout punch. Bessie helped me pick myself up and regain some equilibrium. My father and stepmother were ready to begin a long awaited "round the world in eighty days" trip. Not daring to tell my father, not wanting to intrude on their plans, Bessie was cast into the role of person-who-runs-the-distance. Someone once said the hero is the one who hangs on thirty seconds longer. For the next sixteen years, until her death in 1978, Bessie not only hung in for me, she provided a still vivid portrait of how the injunction "just go on" may be the greatest epitaph by which any of us can hope to be remembered.

During those intervening years, Bessie continued to fashion feathers for me until her eyesight faltered and finally failed. She adored her two grandchildren, and in her usual method of combating the enemy, flew from Illinois to Maryland to visit on three different occasions. With much help from her husband Don she somehow boarded a plane, wheeled into a car, put on her dark glasses so the light did not bother her eyes too much and proceeded to charm her grandchildren and everyone else she met along the way.

I remember all of us visiting my family's weekend home in Oxford, Maryland. Because of the steps, Bessie and I spent several nights in a motel in Easton. After Bessie spent a day wheeling along the brick sidewalks in Oxford, boarding the ferry that traversed the Tred Avon River, having a first-time soft-shell crab at a local fish house, and renaming my youngest son "Why" (although his speech was garbled, the one word that was constant and clear was "why"), the two of us returned to Easton. During the middle of the night, Bessie called to me to get some orange juice. She was experiencing some severe diabetic problems. I remember the fear I felt as clearly as I remember her absolute calmness in the face of what, to her, was a minor setback. Now that I look back, I realize that therein is the key to all our stories. When one is blessed with the ability to just go on, setbacks are only small hurdles. As long as we are willing to wheel when we can no longer walk, to use whatever dark glasses we need to ward off lights that can endanger us, and meet our first soft-shell crab--even though we cannot see it--without preconceived gastronome beliefs, life is truly worth the trip.

I shall always remember Bessie's trip as a "Profile in Courage." When she could no longer see, she continued to bake her notoriously wicked goodies by feeling the ingredients. When she could no longer play the organ, she bought a canary and they sang together. When she could no longer walk the stairs in her home, she sat on them, using her hands to guide her from top to bottom and then reversed the course. When she could no longer run the distance, she not only wheeled it but made "wheelies" to entertain her grandchildren. She was never willing to concede defeat. She was, however, willing to hang on thirty seconds longer.

What Bessie gave me was what I know now, decades later, to be an invaluable gift. She loved me for the "because ofs" and also for all the "in spite ofs" that mothering requires. She accepted me for what I was, and in doing so provided me with a viable example of the limitless boundaries of love. She helped me, through her example, not only to understand courage, but also-- for the first time--etched into my photograph album a picture of "mother." For this I shall always be grateful.

I Never Sang for My Mother

It's been forty-six years since my mother died. I waited forty-five years before I started to search for the person behind the cough, the person not outlined by the coverlet on the bed, the person I cannot remember calling "mother."

We share the same name: She was Elizabeth Lloyd Walter; I am Elizabeth Lloyd Walter. Born in Delta, PA. in 1903, she added the Walter when she married my father in 1929. I was named for her at my birth in 1932. She died a Walter; I was legally reborn last year when I reclaimed the name Walter. Now, I must meet the other Betty, the mother Betty, that shadowy figure I have not allowed to cross over the barriers of time. There is a broken link in my connectiveness. There is a void that perhaps only the first Betty can fill.

In order to begin to remove the barrier to the gate of my memory I must first recreate a picture of my mother. Tennessee Williams said, "In memory everything is played to music." What music should accompany this specter? Only the violin could possibly provide the haunting background that conveys the profound sadness that was her mantra. After all these decades, I suddenly realize I hear no laughter interspersed in her composition. I still hear only the coughing.

My mother was an almost-beautiful woman. There was a softness about her that even the unrelenting tuberculosis could not destroy. When I started my search for the person behind the one picture I have, I began with audiotaped memories from my Aunt Maude, my father's only remaining sister. Traveling to Princeton, New Jersey last November, my friend Sharlene and I listened to and recorded Maude's rambling epiphany. She spoke of my mother's illness that began before she married my father; the tuberculosis was not diagnosed until shortly after my birth. She spoke of her "sweetness" that often could cover a willful nature. She spoke of all the things I already knew. She never spoke of what I am searching for: the key to unlock the door to her spirit and thereby open the door to my understanding.

My first distinct memory of my mother takes place in the living room of the big house in Glen Burnie. This is an important point of reference because the setting--so often the case--is a major character in our play. My father, against all odds, built a beautiful colonial home on Crain Highway in 1932. Starting as a young, very poor, dentist in 1929, he had somehow managed to build the home of his dreams in the midst of the Depression. It was not, however, the home of my mother's dreams. For whatever reasons, she hated my father's monument. For reasons of illness, she was seldom there. Mt. Wilson Sanatorium on Reisterstown Road was her home-away-from-home.

I must have been about four years old when this first flash was developed in the dark room of my memory. It was a Sunday afternoon. One of our many transient "maids" was preparing the Sunday chicken. My mother was on the sofa, my father on a chair by the window. With what I perceive with utter clarity, I said, "Why can't I have a baby brother or sister?" My mother started to cry. I, of course, did not know why.

75

There are two terribly important truths here. One highlights my very early intuitive need *not* to be an only child. Did I know in some deep recess of my psyche that a brother or sister would somehow even up the equation? The truth for me in this memory is that almost sixty years later the need is still there. The far more important element extracted from that hazy recollection is what might have been a later development with my mother. After her death, I was sifting through letters from her sister Ellen. In one, Ellen sent her sympathy for the unfortunate termination of my mother's pregnancy at seven months. The child was dead. The letter was dated June of 1938. This was two years after the first picture in my mother's album and one year before she went to Trudeau Sanatorium in Lake Placid where she would stay for the next five years. The death of the seven-month fetus had never been mentioned, not by anyone. I never questioned my father; I would not have presumed to do so. Secrets were a large part of our family dynamic. They did not add to our success. If the big house was built against all odds, this pregnancy has to be equated in the same manner. Except in this case the odds won. Could my childish plea/question have been part of this decision? Or, in trying to record my memory version of the past, do I struggle with straws and drop them all? All the players are dead. There is no one to validate the memory; no one to tell me what I want to hear: "She loved you so much she risked it all to give you what you wanted most." I am far too old for fairy tales.

Until I wrote, "I hear no laughter" in my mother's picture, I had never thought about that lack. Now that I have removed this vital instrument from the life that I am orchestrating, does this mean I have discovered a truth? No, I have only unearthed a memory.

Another vivid memory takes place at Mt. Wilson Sanatorium. Told to "wait on the steps," I did as directed. "Only" children tend to do as told. Our greatest fear is rooted in even the possibility of displeasing others. I was sixish, and apparently became skittish, letting out a piercing scream that got immediate results. My father appeared, terrified and angry. My mother appeared at the window, terrified. I don't remember her ever being angry. I can, however, still see her face at the window. My father let me know how I had upset my mother. What was I thinking of? She was sick. He was angry. I was bad. I tried never to upset my mother again. I was not always successful.

Thus are our lessons learned. There are no villains here except for what was the common enemy: tuberculosis. Having no drugs to combat the foe, doctors decreed, or agreed, that a stay at Trudeau was the best course of inaction. Fresh, cold air and rest were the antidotes of the time. At least they did no harm.

The evening my mother left, her occasionally occupied bed in the front room of the big house had already been claimed by my father's father, my long-absent grandfather Harry Walter. Dying had driven him back into the bosom of his family. For whatever reasons revolving around family leadership coupled with dormant filial responsibility, my father provided the bedroom. His sister Bess, my new caretaker, Harry's undutiful daughter, provided the toting and fetching. Unwillingly. My memory is of my mother standing on the front porch, crying. Bess did not come to bid goodbye since she and my mother had never, as we used to say, "seen eye to eye." Translation: They intensely disliked each other. I was seven. My mother undoubtedly wanted to kiss me goodbye. Doctors decreed, presumably, that she should not. Touching with tuberculosis was disallowed. That was the credo I most remember. Don't touch. It would take me years to realize that touching need not be dangerous, that love was not a disease, and that contagiously transmitted emotions could be just as dangerous as the microorganism whose presence we tried to avoid.

Some of the best times of my childhood were spent in Lake Placid. Every Christmas my father and I took the train from Penn Station in Baltimore, boarded an overnight sleeper in New York and arrived at Lake Placid. My mother would join us in a hotel in either Saranac Lake or a bed and breakfast-type place at Lake Placid. It is the latter I remember most vividly. The room was festooned (does anyone every use that word today?) with Christmas ornaments, a tree and naturally lots of presents for Betty 2. It started to look just like Christmas; it started to feel just like family. And what does a family "feel" like? Safe.

Although my mother was never able to join us in my abortive attempts at either ice skating or skiing, she was there to listen to the tales of "almost made it around the rink" or "fell only once going down the slope." My father was the one who was the bystander at the largest skating rink *in the world*. I'm sure that distinction is long gone. But so is my most treasured Christmas gift of all. My mother had gotten for me a skating outfit. The jacket was of a red quilted material, the skirt swung out as skaters skirts are wont to do, and the cap was the only "cute cap" I had ever seen. She had found the ideal gift. I'm sure my mother gave me other tangible gifts, but this is the only one I remember.

We also visited on the Fourth of July, but those times are hazy. My mother is more shadowy. Maybe the light was brighter, maybe the exquisite snow and the piercing cold of December are more penetrable in my memory. Maybe she was less energized in the heat of even a Lake Placid July. Maybe it doesn't matter.

When I was eleven, my mother gave up on cold air, gave up on the group housing at the Trudeau year-round campus, and came home. Another crying scene: Mother, Father, Bess the Caretaker, and Betty 2 at the table in the dining room. "Something" was said. I rather imagine anything Bess said would have brought about this reaction on my mother's part. She ran upstairs; I ran after her. She cried; I joined her in her tears. We had a new enemy. She could be seen and she had a name: Bess. Did Bess deserve this? Probably not. Interwoven into this tapestry of tears and recriminations was a long history of rage at her disease, jealousy at Bess's apparent wellness, anger at my father for urging her to return to Trudeau, and I imagine a genuine desire to get to know her daughter. Perhaps I was as shadowy to her as she was to me. Today I understand her rage. At eleven, all this confusion over loyalties, loneliness and love merely spelled turmoil. Of course, today these powerful ingredients still make a wicked stew.

Much whispering behind closed doors, many visits to various doctors who clucked as they examined me, a visit to the local Episcopalian minister who years later would have the honor of pronouncing me a wife for the first time. Then the decision was reached. Bess would go home, my mother would come back to the front bedroom and reclaim her bed, and I would go to Hannah More to be safe from the germs that were our permanent guests. During these long months of agonized decision-making, I had no idea what was afoot. How did I respond when I got wind of the change in the weather? Truthfully, I don't remember. I do remember my first-year response to Hannah More, and that is where my mother and I ran into some serious storms.

I hated everything about the boarding school atmosphere, and in my eleven-year-old (or was I twelve?) lack of either wisdom, perspective or anything bordering on understanding, I hated my mother. Now I remember the age puzzlement. I turned twelve after Christmas of my first unconditionally miserable first year. Pogo was still a raccoon; Walt Kelly had not given him the power of speech. He had not uttered those immortal words, "We have met the enemy and he is us." I would not have understood them even if he had. Do any of us comprehend the sageness of Pogo until we have been through our own crucible and somehow remain standing? No.

I would not speak to my mother when she called, so my father was the one left holding the receiver. What torment this must have been for her. What agony my father must have withstood, torn between a wretchedly miserable whiny child and an equally miserable ill wife. Sometime between September and Christmas, my father had one of his "heart-to-hearters" with me. Somehow, he was able to get across, through or beyond me and into the "situation." By some miracle, I must have gotten some inkling of the distress I was causing. The drug of pleasing is far more powerful than the drug of distancing. Naturally, I chose pleasing. It was not only a family role; it was one that I was most comfortable in. To this day, hurting another person is devastating to me. As I see this in print, I wonder if my brief role as hater had longer-lasting effects than I might have imagined.

There are other longer-lasting effects of my shorter-distanced relationship with my mother from 1944 to 1948. Routinely, they came to visit every Thursday afternoon and every Sunday. After a while, "they" became "he": my father. My mother, more often than not, could not make the journey from Glen Burnie to Reisterstown. She could, however, make the journey to Hutzler's bake shop. From there, she ordered to be sent on a regular basis the most wonderful chocolate cake ever baked in the history of chocolate kind. This arrived every Friday, boxed by the Hutzler's boxers, and crumbled beyond recognition...but not taste! This became an anticipated event, and I held the power of deciding which girls would share in this treat-to-end-all-treats. I made many short-term friends in this fashion!

Apparently, my mother had a standing order at the bakers. If she couldn't make it, she called. God knows how many cakes showed up on her Hutzler's charge card. I have a love affair with chocolate that transcends the usual chocolate lover's rapture. Chocolate is comforting, chocolate is good, chocolate is nurturing. Chocolate is mother? Recently, when I joined some of my long-ago Hannah More friends for an Annapolis luncheon, they first talked to me about their still remembered love for my father. Then they laughed about the cakes we all looked forward to, and memories of my mother.

The summers are very vague to me. My mother was constantly abed. I consistently went to summer school due to failing math grades. The big house was always quiet, many part-time nurse types wafted in and out and I fell out of love with chocolate (temporarily!) and in love with the movies. Three times a week the movie changed at the new Glen Theater. Three times a week I was there, eleven cents in hand, to watch life as seen through the eyes of John Wayne, June Allyson, Van Johnson,

John Payne, Anne Baxter, Bette Davis, Cornel Wilde, Lana Turner, Joan Crawford and.... Errol Flynn's "Robin Hood" was more seductive than any candy bar ever conceived! I would go home and knock on my mother's door, go in, position myself across the room so I did not have to face the germ directly and pour out my girlish dreams of one day meeting Errol Flynn, or Glenn Ford, or Tyrone Power, or....! She listened. She may even have smiled, but you know what? She never laughed. Maybe not laughing can be a good thing?

It was years later that I questioned why I could go home during the summers but not stay there during the year. Was the enemy dormant during the summer? Our room had an adjoining door, so crying and coughing were easily heard. I escaped to the movies during the day and to books at night. A book a day keeps the questions away? Like the movies, the library was open only three evenings a week. My friend Pat Reynolds and I went every night it was open, got three books each and repaired to our respective rooms to read. Between the romanticism of the movies of the forties and the glorification or romance that those three-name lady writers eschewed, is it any wonder so many of us found the life in the real lane so disenchanting?

During the summer of 1948 I was retaking geometry at yet another summer school in Baltimore City. My mother died on a Monday night. I remember it was Monday because I had seen a film with Clark Gable and Lana Turner on Sunday afternoon. A real tear-jerker, even I knew it was pretty awful. As I was walking home, something felt, well, "off." A premonition? The house was quieter than usual. My father was agitated; my mother's legs were terribly swollen. A doctor came. The doors remained closed. I read my book and tried not to listen. I had become quite adept at not hearing.

The death day started out as usual. I went to geometry school; I was very nervous. Of course I knew. The wings of the Angel of Death make a whirring sound, a sound like hummingbirds that have been miked. Once you hear their music

81

it is forever imprinted on the recorder in your memory. During class, I received a call from my father. I was to stay in the city and see a movie. As I recall, I asked no questions, made no attempt to find out the "why." I merely left my book behind and trudged off to the Stanley Theater. To my credit, I do not remember what movie took up those two hours.

When I arrived home, Ellen was there with her friend Mrs. Davis. Georgia Davis was a lovely, very wealthy, very cultured and may I add, very kind woman. It was she who told me that my mother was dying. I was sixteen years old.

And what did I feel; how did I react? I vaguely remember asking if I should go in and see her. My father said that was not a good idea. I was immensely relieved. That night I went to bed in the adjoining room. Self-taught not to hear, I must have slept because the next picture is distinct. I awoke to hear Ellen making the funeral arrangements on the telephone that was on the bedstand next to the bed. I was told to go to Pat Reynold's house and stay there. The body had to be removed; the coughing had been silenced.

The funeral was on a Wednesday at the Harkins Funeral Home in Delta, PA. My mother was buried at Slate Ridge Cemetery outside of Delta. I remembered her grave as being on a hill with a beautiful tree overhead. I remembered incorrectly. Last August I planned to visit my mother's sister, Mary Williams. I had delayed the visit on three separate occasions. You understand, we busy people have so many irons in so many fires that we always run the chance of getting severely burned. This turned out to be one of those burning times. I called Mary on a Tuesday morning in August to tell her that finally my friend Sharlene (who always seems to accompany me on trips of import) and I were coming up on Thursday. I called twice that morning and as I listened to the unanswered rings, I knew I had called too late. When I called again at 1:30 that afternoon, my cousin Jan Marie told me that her mother had died that morning. The questions I had wanted to ask Mary about my mother remain unanswered. Could she have given me another key? Maybe.

My friend and I went to visit on Thursday as planned. I reconnected with long removed cousins, all of whom were warm and gracious. When I went out on the porch to smoke a cigarette, Evelyn said, "Don't tell me you smoke! Don't you remember your mother and Ellen? Shame on you." Yes, well...shame on all of us. Did I forget to mention that one association I always carried of my mother was Pall Mall cigarettes? Ah, a slip of memory? Did I forget to mention that my preferred nicotine of choice happens to be Benson and Hedges? And may I mention that one of my least favorite lines happens to be "Shame on you"? I will swear on my mother's grave (a fitting symbol?) that I have never, nor will I ever say, "Shame on anyone." Let the shamer beware!

Donny, once the baby, recently celebrated his fiftieth birthday. He took us to the cemetery. I had not returned since my mother's funeral. The grave is not on a hill; perhaps the tree was struck by lightning. Perhaps it was removed to make room for more graves. I swear (on my mother's grave?) there *was* a tree. Why is this important? Because I remember my father saying, "She will sleep well here. The tree will protect her." Why is that tree gone?

The tombstone is imposing. The name Elizabeth Lloyd Walter is there. Beloved husband Henry Maynard; beloved daughter, Elizabeth. But there are no dates. Neither birth nor death is chiseled in stone. I know I must do this. I must give, in stone, beginning and end to her life. In so doing, I must acknowledge her beginning and end in my life.

There is a play entitled, "I Never Sang for My Father." I've never understood why I always tear up when I hear those words. Now I know. It is because I never sang for my mother. Perhaps I can do it now.

Made in the USA
Charleston, SC
31 December 2016